Reading Bridge™

Written by:

Jennifer Moore

Project Directors: Michele D. Van Leeuwen
                          Scott G. Van Leeuwen

**Creative & Marketing
Director:**   George Starks

**Product Development
& Design Director:**   Dante J. Orazzi

Reading Bridge™
4th Grade

For more information write or call:
Rainbow Bridge Publishing
332 West Martin Lane
Salt Lake City, UT 84107
801-268-8887
www.rainbowbridgepub.com

Original Cover Art:
Joe Flores

Proofreaders:
Debbie Armstrong, Angela Erickson, Dante Orazzi, George Starks, Dave Thompson, Carol VanLeeuwen, Kirsten Wille, Dixon

Graphic Design, Illustration and Layout:
Thomas Dyches, Dante Orazzi and Jeffrey Whitehead

The authors would like to gratefully acknowledge the assistance and suggestions of the following persons:
Debbie Armstrong, William Baker, Randy Britton, Harriett Cook, Susan Denissen, Leland Graham, Wade Keung, Darriel Ledbetter, Becky Lee, Gina Monteleone, Beverly Moody, Melanie Moore, Lee Orr, Dan Payne, Dianne Sims, and John Spilane.

Printed by Press America in the U.S.A.

Printing History:
First Printing 1999
Second Printing 2000

ISBN: 1-887923-11-X

Printed in the United States of America
10 9 8 7 6 5 4 3 2 1

TABLE OF CONTENTS

Introduction

The **Reading Bridge** series is designed to improve and motivate students' reading. This book has been developed to provide fourth grade students practical skill-based exercises in the areas of inferences, main ideas, cause and effect, fact and opinion, and figurative language. The purpose of this book is to familiarize students with the kinds of reading tasks they will encounter on a daily basis. Furthermore, reading will enrich and facilitate their lives as young adults in an ever-changing world that has information readily available but only if they learn to take advantage of and appreciate reading.

The stories, poems, essays and puzzles in this collection are each accompanied by exercises that address reading skills. Each story, poem or essay has been written so that students at the fourth grade level can read it successfully. The carefully thought-out questions will help your students learn to think, inquire, create, imagine, respond and in some instances, do research to learn more about a specific topic.

Reading Bridge adapts to any teaching situation whether at home or in the classroom. It can be used in many different ways. For instance:

✔ **For at home practice:** this series is ideal to supplement or extend school work and home school reading programs.

✔ **For the entire class:** this series can be used for intensive reinforcement of reading skills or to simply supplement a basal reading program.

✔ **For reading groups:** this series will provide skills practice at appropriate levels, and the reading exercises become progressively more challenging.

✔ **For individual use:** this series will help build a completely individualized program.

Use Your Dictionary!!!

The English language is made up of thousands and thousands and thousands of words; so many words that it would be impossible for you to know what every single one of these words means! But wait! Just because you come across a word in this book, or somewhere else, that may be unfamiliar to you, does not mean that you should ignore it or give up on learning its meaning.

Instead, use a dictionary to learn the meaning of the word you don't know. You'll get better scores on the exercises in this book. More importantly, you'll expand your knowledge base and become a better communicator because you'll be able to both express yourself and understand other people more clearly!

Dic • tion • ar • y, n. **1.** a book of alphabetically listed words in a language, with definitions, pronunciations, and other information about the words

4th Grade Reading List

Ballard, Robert D.
Finding the Titanic

Cleary, Beverly
Dear Mr. Henshaw
Ellen Tebbits
Emily's Runaway Imagination
Henry and Ribsy
Henry and the Paper Route
Henry Huggins
Muggie Maggie
Otis Spofford

Cole, Joanna
The Magic School Bus books
At the Waterworks
Hops Home
In the Haunted Museum
Inside the Earth
Inside the Human Body
Lost In the Solar System
On the Ocean Floor

Dahl, Roald
Charlie and the Chocolate Factory
Charlie and the Great Glass Elevator
Fantastic Mr. Fox
George's Marvelous Medicine
Matilda
Witches

Dixon, Franklin W.
Hardy Boys Mysteries
Bombay Boomerang
Danger on Vampire Trail
Haunted Fort
Hunting For Hidden Gold
Mysterious Caravan
Mystery of the Cabin Island
Mystery of the Whale Tattoo
Pentagon Spy

Secret of the Caves
Secret of the Old Mill

Doyle, Sir Arthur Conan
Sherlock Holmes Mysteries
Adventures of the Empty House
Adventures of the Speckled Band
Final Problem

Estes, Eleanor Ruth
Hundred Dresses

Ferguson, Alane
Cricket and the Crackerbox Kid

Fitzgerald, John Dennis
Great Brain
Great Brain at the Academy
Great Brain Does it Again
Great Brain Reforms
Return of the Great Brain

Grove, Vicki
Good-Bye My Wishing Star

Hass, E. A.
Incognito Mosquito
Incognito Mosquito Flies Again
Incognito Mosquito, Private Insective

Keene, Carolyn
Nancy Drew Mysteries
Case of the Disappearing Diamonds
Clue to the Crumbling Wall
Double Jinx Mystery
Emerald-Eyed Cat Mystery
Enemy Match
Eskimo's Secret
Ghost of Blackwood Hall
Haunted Carousel
Mardi Gras Mystery
Secret in the Old Attic

4th Grade Reading List

Kingfisher Publications
    1,000 Facts about People
    1,000 Facts about Space
    1,000 Facts about Wild Animals
    Forest Animals
    Polar Animals
    Seashore Animals

Korman, Susan
    Alien Alert

Lowry, Lois
    All About Sam
    Anastasia Krupnik series

MacDonald, Kate
    Anne of Green Gables Cookbook

Mills, Lauren R.
    Rag Coat

Money, Walt
    Gentle Ben
    Kavik, the Wolf Dog

Paulsen, Gary
    Dunc and Amos Hit the Big Top
    Dunc and the Flaming Ghost
    Dunc Breaks the Record
    Dunc Gets Tweaked
    Hatchet
    Escape from Fire Mountain
    Legend of Red Horse Cavern
    Rodomonte's Revenge
    Wild Culpepper Cruise

Peet, Bill
    Bill Peet: An Autobiography

Sachar, Louis
    There's a Boy in the Girls' Bathroom
    Sideways Stories From Wayside School

Schulz, Charles
    For the Love of Peanuts

Sobol, Donald J.
    Encyclopedia Brown series
    Boy Detective
    Case of the Dead Eagles
    Case of the Disgusting Sneakers
    Case of the Midnight Visitor
    Case of the Mysterious Handprints
    Case of the Secret Pitch
    Case of the Treasure Hunt
    Case of the Two Spies
    Find the Clues
    Gets His Man
    Keeps the Peace
    Lends a Hand
    Sets the Pace
    Shows the Way
    Takes the Cake
    Tracks them Down

Speare, Elizabeth George
    Calico Captive
    Sign of the Beaver

Stamm, Claus
    Three Strong Women

Thomas, Jane Resh
    Comeback Dog

Warner, Gertrude Chandler
    Boxcar Children books
    Blue Bay Mystery
    Yellow House
    Lighthouse Mystery
    Mike's Mystery
    Mystery Ranch
    Surprise Island
    Woodshed Mystery

Incentive Contract

In • cen'tive, n. 1. Something that urges a person on. 2. Enticing. 3. Encouraging 4. That which excites to action or moves the mind.

Below, List Your Agreed-Upon Incentive for Each Story Group

Student's Signature _____ **Parent, Teacher, or Guardian Signature** _____

Place a ✔ after each story & exercise upon completion

Page	Story & Exercise Title	✔	Page	Story & Exercise Title	✔
8	Mars		44	Spirit in Baseball	
10	Pet Sitters Club		47	Visitors Poem	
11	Todd's Birthday		49	Ski School	
12	Amazing Amphibians		53	The Ice Cream Shop	
13	Won Ton Soup		56	Kelly's Lesson	
14	Keeping it Green		58	Maggie's New House	
15	Limerick		60	Jessica's New Room	
16	A Boat Ride in the Keys		64	A New Puppy	
17	The Red Cross		66	Sarah's Dinner	
18	The Boys of Third Grade		68	Zoo Helpers	
19	The Airport		71	Christmas	
20	Homework		72	The Hike Poem	

My Incentive Is

My Incentive Is

Page	Story & Exercise Title	✔	Page	Story & Exercise Title	✔
21	Money		73	Sand People Poem	
23	King Arthur		74	Valentine Cookies	
24	President Abraham Lincoln		77	Surfing The Web	
26	Libraries		79	A Visit With Matisse	
27	Computers		80	Have Some Tea	
29	Math		81	Art Lessons	
31	The Making of a Movie		83	London	
32	The Reading Contest		85	Jimmy's Candy Shop Adventure	
34	Rock Hounds		88	Natalie's Secret Place	
37	The Patriots		90	Science Matters	
39	Jenny's Vacation		91	Daniel's Holiday	
42	The Ballet Swan		93	Mile High City	

My Incentive Is

My Incentive Is

Some people call it the red planet because, from Earth, it appears to have a red color. We can see Mars, our neighbor in the solar system, without a telescope. Earth is the third closest planet to the sun and Mars is the fourth.

Scientists have found that the conditions on Mars are most similar to Earth's than any of the other planets.

Mars has an oval shaped orbit path and takes about 687 earth days to move around the sun. We know Earth takes 365 days, or one year, to orbit the sun. Mars, like Earth, rotates on an imaginary axis. It has an atmosphere of mostly carbon dioxide and very little oxygen. There is very little water we know of on Mars, but still some scientists believe there is some form of life there.

MARS

READING CHALLENGE

After reading "Mars," answer the following questions.

1. **Mars is a _____ in our solar system.**
   A. sun   B. star   C. planet   D. galaxy

2. **From Earth, Mars appears to be a _____ color.**
   A. red   B. blue   C. white   D. black

3. **Mars has an orbit path that is a(n) _____ shape.**
   A. round   B. oval   C. straight   D. square

4. **The conditions on Mars are most similar to this planet.**
   A. Neptune   B. Earth   C. Mercury   D. Venus

5. **There is very little _____ on Mars.**
   A. weather   B. water   C. time   D. heat

8   **Total Correct_____**

THE CROSSWORD CHALLENGE
SOLAR SYSTEM PUZZLE

ACROSS

4. A ball of heat in the center of the universe.
5. A heavenly body with a head and a tail.
7. A planet's satellite.
9. A device used for looking at stars.

DOWN

1. The planet with rings.
2. The far planet.
3. The path a planet follows.
6. The planet we live on.
7. The closest planet to the sun.
8. A band of stars.

Total Correct _____

THE PET SITTERS CLUB

Becky and Lisa live on the same street and both have dogs. Lisa also has a cat. They have trained their dogs to walk on a leash, play ball, and do some tricks. Lisa's cat will ride in her bicycle basket. Many neighbors have seen their kindness toward the pets and are impressed. One day a neighbor suggested the girls start a pet sitting business for the neighborhood. Becky and Lisa liked the idea and decided to get started immediately.

The girls began their enterprise by making fancy flyers on Becky's computer. They listed the services of "The Pet Sitters Club": dog walking, over-night pet sitting, grooming and dog training. They hopped on their bikes and started distributing the flyers. Soon every mailbox in the neighborhood had a flyer on it. Calls started coming in requesting services from the Pet Sitters Club.

During the first week, the girls received about four jobs a day. The second week business increased to six jobs per day. They worked five days. The Pet Sitters Club received a lot of praise from the neighbors and the girls were thrilled. The summer seemed to pass quickly and Becky and Lisa were pleased with their success. They decided to send notes to the neighbors, thanking them for their business. They reminded their clients to look for the Pet Sitters Club to return next summer.

READING CHALLENGE

After reading "The Pet Sitters Club," answer the following questions.

---

1. **The girls began a pet care business because they needed extra money.**
   A. true   B. false

2. **The Pet Sitters Club was started by Becky and Lisa.**
   A. true   B. false

3. **The girls designed flyers using Lisa's computer.**
   A. true   B. false

4. **What was the main reason the girls started the Pet Sitters club?**
   A. to help stray animals   B. to earn extra money
   C. to have fun with animals   D. to please their parents

5. **How many pets did the girls care for in their second week of work?**
   A. 4   B. 6   C. 30   D. 28

RBP

Total Correct_____

Todd's Birthday

On Saturday, Todd Hambidge will be thirteen years old. He is excited about this particular birthday because he is going deer hunting with his dad and Uncle Mike. He was very glad that his father had been careful to teach him about gun safety and hunting. Todd has discovered hunting is more about listening and watching than shooting at things. He has learned these lessons well and is ready for the great outdoors. He and his dad plan to leave early on Saturday in order to get to the tree stand and establish the watch for the day.

Uncle Mike will meet them at the Quick Stop gas station. They'll leave for the woods together. Uncle Mike will carry the knapsack with the food, water and other necessities. Todd is well prepared for this outing. He knows to be a courteous hunter and respect the privilege of hunting and bringing in food for the family. He remembers studying in school about the Indian's way of using the animal as completely as possible. He likes that idea because it is responsible.

Reckless poachers who destroy animals to make money from the skins or other parts annoy Todd. He realizes they violate laws and he knows that is wrong. Saturday will be a milestone birthday in many ways. Todd will be a teenager and he will be his dad's hunting partner.

READING CHALLENGE

After reading "Todd's Birthday," answer the following questions.

---

1. **Todd is excited about this birthday most, because**
   - A. he'll be able to have a gun.
   - B. he'll be a teenager.
   - C. he'll be his dad's hunting partner.
   - D. he'll cook dinner for the family.

2. **Uncle Mike is going with Todd and his father because**
   - A. he needs to get gas in his truck.
   - B. he enjoys hunting.
   - C. he will teach Todd how to hunt.
   - D. he is an Indian.

3. **What does the author mean by the term "milestone?"**
   - A. a rock in the road found each mile
   - B. a unit of measure hunters use
   - C. a way to check how far you walked
   - D. a date or event that is special

4. **How does Todd feel about the opportunity to go hunting?**

AMAZING AMPHIBIANS

Able to leap lily pads in a single bound! Sounds rather like a super-hero than a frog. Well, thanks to their strong back legs these little green friends are quite agile and helpful. Since frogs live on insects, that makes our life a bit more pleasant. Frogs are cold-blooded animals and usually become inactive, or even hibernate in winter. The average frog can jump about two feet, but some bullfrogs have been

known to jump distances of approximately six feet.

Man is the frog's most feared enemy. Humans use frogs often in scientific study because of their intricate body systems. Frogs are delicious to birds, snakes and some people consider frog legs quite a treat. Frogs are small animals with bulging eyes and croaking voices. Not all frogs live in water. However, frogs are considered amphibians because they do spend at least some of their time in the water.

READING CHALLENGE

After reading "Amazing Amphibians," answer the following questions.

1. **What do frogs eat?**
   A. grass   B. insects   C. spiders   D. all plants

2. **What body part of the frog is especially adapted for jumping?**
   A. legs   B. neck   C. feet   D. arms

3. **Which type of frogs can jump the longest distances?**
   A. tree frogs   B. green frogs   C. bullfrogs   D. grass frogs

4. **What reason did the author give that indicated humans are the frog's enemy?**
   A. Humans attempt to keep food away from frogs.
   B. Humans use frogs for scientific study.
   C. Humans use frogs for pets.
   D. Humans use frogs for fishing bait.

5. **Which word did the author use to describe the eyes of the frog?**
   A. large   B. bulging   C. round   D. crooked

Won Ton Soup

Lin Yi was ten years old when her family moved to the United States from China. She was excited about coming to the United States, but a little nervous too. In China she always had her grandmother's homemade won ton soup. Lin enjoyed helping her grandmother make the soup and she would miss that.

In the United States, Lin met an American girl in her class named Jennifer. Lin liked going to Jennifer's house and having pizza, popcorn and watching movies. Sometimes Lin would spend the night with Jennifer too. Lin's family did not have a television or a video cassette player yet. Her father and mother were trying to get the necessities in the house first. Lin had just gotten her new bed. Later she would get a television.

One day, Lin invited Jennifer over while her mother was making several Chinese foods for dinner. One of the things she made was the delicious won ton soup her grandmother often made. Mrs. Yi was working on the noodles while Jennifer and Lin measured the water and cut up the onions for the broth. Soon each of them had their part finished and the soup was placed on the stove to cook. Then Mr. Yi came in and complimented the cooks on the wonderful smell.

When the soup was ready, the girls prepared the table and Lin brought the chop sticks to the table. Jennifer was surprised that she was going to have to eat with chop sticks! Mrs. Yi placed the rice, pork and a platter of mixed Chinese vegetables on the table. Lin served the soup into bowls. The family sat down with their American guest and began eating. Jennifer was good at using the chopsticks and the soup was excellent. This was great fun and the Yi family was very happy to share their stories of China and their trip west that evening at dinner. Lin decided that her grandmother would be proud of the soup. It really was good.

READING CHALLENGE

After reading "Won Ton Soup," answer the following questions.

1. What country is Jennifer's friend from?

2. What foods do the girls eat at Jennifer's house?

3. How many different foods did Lin's mother make the night Jennifer visited for dinner?

4. Why did the author say the Yi family had a "western," journey when they came to America?

Keeping It Green

William and Tommy were in the fifth grade together and they lived on the same street. Tommy's father and mother seemed to always be in their yard planting flowers and doing different projects to make the yard look better. William had been riding bikes with Tommy one afternoon when they saw Tommy's parents outside working, again! They stopped to talk and asked if there was anything they could help do. Tommy's dad looked around and said it would be great to have some help spreading mulch, watering and raking the flower beds.

After an hour, the boys were very hot and ready for a drink of water. Tommy's mom had a pitcher of water on the patio table and some cups. The boys drank quickly and had refills. There were only four flower beds that needed to be finished. Tommy began working again and asked his father why gardening was so important to him. He carefully explained to Tommy that it is about keeping the property green, or in other words, healthy. It is good for the soil to plant things and it is good to grow things because the beauty of nature makes the world a little nicer, his dad said. William was impressed with the answer Tommy's dad gave and he decided to encourage his parents to do more gardening.

READING CHALLENGE

After reading "Keeping it Green," answer the following questions.

---

1. **What grade are William and Tommy in at school?**
   A. second   B. fourth   C. fifth   D. sixth

2. **What projects do Tommy's parents often do?**
   A. building   B. gardening   C. painting   D. cleaning

3. **How long did the boys work before they stopped for a water break?**
   A. one hour   B. thirty minutes   C. two hours   D. four hours

4. **After the break, the boys had _____ flower beds to finish.**
   A. 3   B. 5   C. 2   D. 4

5. **In your own words, explain the main idea of this paragraph.**

Total Correct _____

RBP

Limerick

The limerick is a five-line, humorous verse that is written so that the first, second and fifth lines rhyme. The third and fourth lines carry on the idea of the verse and provide another rhyme. Edward Lear made the limerick famous in the 1800's with his humorous verses. Look over the limerick written below to see what the author is using for humor.

Homework's a chore.

If it weren't such a bore.

I guess I can manage.

So I get the advantage.

Perhaps it's the math I deplore.

READING CHALLENGE

After reading "Limerick," answer the following questions.

1. **What is the author writing about in this limerick?**
   A. math   B. boring things   C. homework   D. can't tell

2. **What is the author comparing homework to?**
   A. math   B. cleaning   C. boring things   D. nothing

3. **What do you think the writer of this limerick thinks about math? Explain in your own words in the space below.**

A Boat Ride in the Keys

Sam and his family went on a vacation to the Florida Keys. They had been to several beaches before but none that had water like this. The water was so clear that Sam could see the fish swimming below the surface of the water.

Sam and his family took a ride in a glass bottom boat. The tour guide on the boat gave each passenger a reference card with pictures of different types of fish on it. As the boat traveled through the water, the passengers could see the fish in the water beneath the boat. Sam had a lot of fun using his card to identify the fish he saw.

Soon the tour was over and the guide helped everyone get off the boat. Sam was very happy that he was near the back of the boat so he could wait longer than the other passengers to get off. The fish were swimming all around and Sam counted seven different kinds of fish. He was very pleased with his "underwater," study, and he didn't even have to get wet!

READING CHALLENGE

After reading "A Boat Ride in the Keys," answer the following questions.

1. **Sam and his family went on vacation to a _____.**
   A. desert
   B. mountain
   C. river
   D. beach

2. **Sam was fascinated by the _____.**
   A. wildlife
   B. sand
   C. fish
   D. people

3. **The tour guide was on the _____.**
   A. mountain hike
   B. nature trail
   C. glass-bottom boat
   D. beach

4. **Why was Sam glad to be the last one off the boat?**
   A. Because he was sick
   B. Because he liked seeing the fish
   C. Because he was getting wet
   D. Because he had more time to eat

5. **How many different kinds of fish did Sam see on his trip?**
   A. 4
   B. 5
   C. 6
   D. 7

Remember, if you don't know what a word means, look it up in a dictionary! You'll do better in the exercises!

 Total Correct_____

THE RED CROSS

The Red Cross is an organization that was established to provide help to people in emergency situations. The main goal is to relieve human suffering. Established in Switzerland in 1863, the Red Cross has a presence in over one hundred nations. The symbolic flag displays a red cross on a white background which honors Switzerland.

The Red Cross offers a variety of programs like: water safety, disaster relief, blood drives, nursing, health, and youth activities. All of the programs are open to the public. The Red Cross is established in major cities across the United States and supported by thousands of part- and full-time volunteers. The budget on which the organization functions is money raised from voluntary donations.

The volunteers who work for the Red Cross are professionals from a variety of careers. Some volunteer teams are made up of high school and college students. They donate their time and expertise to helping others in need. The Red Cross touches many people's lives and helps in a very special way.

READING CHALLENGE

After reading "The Red Cross," answer the following questions.

1. **The Red Cross was established in _____ in 1863.**
   - A. all nations
   - B. the United States
   - C. Switzerland
   - D. Europe

2. **The programs the Red Cross offers include, but aren't limited to :**
   - A. safety, hospital training, blood drives and nurse training.
   - B. water, safety, blood drives, nursing and health programs.
   - C. safety, disaster relief and international politics.
   - D. driver education, disaster plans and hurricanes.

3. **The term "donations," refers to:**
   - A. monetary contributions.
   - B. giving away toys.
   - C. school supplies.
   - D. volunteers.

4. **Volunteer teams can be made up of:**
   - A. adults and children.
   - B. non-working people and students.
   - C. adults and students.
   - D. paid professionals and doctors.

5. **Red Cross societies are in _____ different nations.**
   - A. few
   - B. several
   - C. many
   - D. only four

RBP

The Boys of Third Grade

It was the first day of school and Jacob was very nervous. He was not sure he wanted to be in fourth grade. Third grade was really fun and he liked his teacher, Mrs. Donald, a lot. This year was probably going to be much harder. He was not sure who was going to be in his class or where he would sit at lunch. He decided this was too much to think about all at once.

He quickly got dressed and went downstairs to eat breakfast. His mom and dad were drinking coffee. His father was dressed for work and very chatty about the excitement of the first day of school. Jacob ate his bagel then excused himself to go brush his teeth. He soon returned to get his things and leave for the bus. His parents said good-bye and his mother gave him her usual kiss.

On his way to the bus, Jacob thought about his friends from third grade. Everyone else was going to be a little nervous in fourth grade too. Maybe it would not be so bad. He got on the bus and saw his friends Mark and Jake sitting in the back. They waved to Jacob and asked him to sit with them. On the way to school the boys talked about the new school year and hoped they would be in the same class for their fourth grade year.

The bus arrived at the school and everyone got off and headed for the doors. Jacob entered the fourth grade hall with his friends and they searched the classrooms and finally found their names on the list for Miss Davison's class. They were all three in the same class. Their friend Taylor was in their class too. The boys went inside and sat down near each other and tried to contain their excitement. This was going to be a great year. The best friends of third grade were now in fourth!

READING CHALLENGE

After reading "The Boys of Third Grade," answer the following question.

Respond to each statement by writing "T," for true and "F," for false.

1. _____ The boys were walking to school.
2. _____ Third grade was fun for Jacob.
3. _____ Jacob's fourth grade teacher was Mrs. Donald.
4. _____ Taylor was not in Jacob's fourth grade class.
5. _____ After eating breakfast, Jacob went to brush his teeth.
6. _____ The bus was late getting to the school.
7. _____ Mark and Jake did not want Jacob to sit with them on the bus.
8. _____ Miss Davison teaches the fourth grade.
9. _____ In the last paragraph the word "contain," means to hold inside.
10. _____ "Jacob," and "Jake," refer to the same person.

*Total Correct*_____

The Airport

Mandy Allen was going to Maine to visit her grandparents. She lives with her family in Georgia and every year her family travels to Maine at Thanksgiving to see her grandparents. Mandy arrived at the airport with her family. Mr. Allen went in and presented the tickets to the airline ticket agent at the large white desk. The agent asked them how many suitcases they would be checking. Mandy's father answered the agent and placed the luggage on the low step beside the large desk. The agent was very polite, took the luggage and placed tags on each piece. He returned the tickets to Mr. Allen and told them to have a nice flight.

The Allen family walked down a long hallway to a security booth. The officer at the security booth was checking all incoming passengers for airport security.

Next, they walked on to the gate where they would board the airplane. This looked to Mandy like the waiting room at her dentist's office. Soon a man in a dark uniform and white shirt spoke over the intercom. He called all of the passengers by row numbers. Mandy led the way as her family walked by the man in the uniform. He took their tickets and the Allen family walked through the jet way to the airplane. Mandy was so excited.

READING CHALLENGE

After reading "The Airport," answer the following questions.

Decide if the answer for the blank is "before," or "after."

1. Mandy and her family got their luggage checked in at the desk_____they went through the security check.

2. Mr. Allen gave the ticket to the agent to check in _____they arrived at the airport.

3. Mandy walked down the jet way _____the man in the uniform called her family's row number.

4. Mr. Allen and the family got on the airplane _____they walked down the long hallway.

5. The Allen family waited at the airport gate _____they got on the airplane to go to Maine.

6. Mr. Allen must have bought the tickets _____the family arrived at the airport for the trip.

Homework

John doesn't like to do his homework late at night. He prefers to get all of the assignments done in the afternoon after he gets in from school. John's mother, Mrs. Henry, is a teacher and she is at home after school each day. John and his sister, Kelly, get off of the bus at about three-thirty. If they need help or have a question about their homework, their mom is there to help.

John is proud because he usually can do the work alone. He spends about twenty minutes on his math and thirty minutes on his vocabulary lessons and another fifteen minutes on his science. Sometimes he will not have a science homework assignment and there is a history lesson instead. This is a good schedule for John because it means he is finished by about five o'clock.

After his homework is completely done John calls his friend Zach who lives next door. Zach is a very good student. He's on a soccer team, and is usually at home by four o'clock. The boys play together from five o'clock until six o'clock. Zach's father arrives home by six and John's dad gets home at 6:30. The boys know that they should be inside to have dinner with their families at six, and share their homework with their dads. After dinner they read together or study for a test. John and Zach like spending time with their fathers and presenting their completed homework.

READING CHALLENGE

After reading "Homework," answer the following questions.

1. **How many minutes of vocabulary homework does John usually have?**
   A. thirty
   B. fifteen
   C. twenty
   D. not given

2. **Who is John's next door neighbor?**
   A. Kelly
   B. Zach
   C. Henry
   D. John

3. **What kind of job does John's mother have?**
   A. secretary
   B. chef
   C. teacher
   D. soccer coach

4. **What time does Zach's father usually get home each evening?**
   A. 3:00
   B. 5:00
   C. 6:00
   D. 6:30

5. **Zach and John usually stop playing together after six because**
   A. they have to finish their homework.
   B. their parents want to have them get to bed early.
   C. they eat dinner and visit with their parents.
   D. they like to watch their favorite T.V. shows.

Total Correct_____

Money

Money is something everyone will use at some time. It allows people to buy things and pay for services. In the United States we use dollars and coins for money. In other countries similar paper and metal material is used but it is called by different names. In Great Britain money is called pound sterling. The Japanese call theirs yen.

When people travel to other countries where a different type of money is used, they may exchange their money for the money used in that country. Often there is a difference between the worth of the two types of money. Governments determine the value of the money for their country and they establish an exchange rate for their money to be swapped for another country's money.

Money has a long history because early in our civilization people realized that we needed something to use for valuable trade. Babylonians in the 3000's B.C. used a "due bill" which was a clay stone with the items owed to the merchant listed on the clay. Roman soldiers used to be paid with lumps of salt. Today we occasionally say "he is not worth his salt," which is related to a Roman soldier who did not do a very good job. Surely we want goods and services that are "worth their salt!"

READING CHALLENGE

After reading "Money," answer the following questions.

1. **Japanese money is called _____.**
   A. yen   B. dollar   C. pound   D. bill

2. **Great Britain uses the _____.**
   A. yen   B. dollar   C. pound   D. bill

3. **According to the passage, money is used in society mainly for this purpose:**
   A. To show how wealthy you are so you can brag to others.
   B. Money is how we buy goods and pay for services.
   C. It is the way we use our nation's resources.
   D. Money is used instead of salt.

4. **The Roman soldiers were paid by:**
   A. vacation time.   B. dollars.   C. salt.   D. yen.

5. **Money was invented in civilization for:**
   A. wealth.   B. trade.   C. status.   D. gambling.

THE CROSSWORD CHALLENGE

Money Puzzle

ACROSS

3. A monetary institution.
4. Equal to four quarters.
6. People whose pictures appear on American dollars.
8. Dimes, pennies, nickels, quarters.
9. One-fourth of a dollar.

DOWN

1. A place to keep and carry your money.
2. Metal used for making pennies.
5. Equal to ten pennies.
6. One cent.
7. Twenty makes a dollar.

Total Correct _____

RBP

King Arthur

Legend has it that England once had a noble king named Arthur who fought for good and respectable things. He defeated his foes and won the love and admiration of his countrymen. He held his court in a place called Camelot and his knights sat at a round table. The symbolic round table was to show that they all worked together and no one was at the head of the table. In King Arthur's court, no knight had more responsibility or influence than any other knight. There are many stories of the Middle Ages that hold King Arthur as the hero. He is said to have brought order and peace to his kingdom.

As a child, Arthur discovered his regal legacy when he was the only one who could free a sword that was lodged in a stone outside a cathedral. Arthur's father and mother died when he was young and he was raised by his uncle. With the help of a magician, Merlin, he was guided to his destiny. He later married the beautiful Guinevere, whom he loved deeply. He and his knights were known for their kindness and gentleness, or chivalry. He received a gift from the "Lady of the Lake," his famous sword, Excalibur. This was the sword he used in battle many times. Legend says Arthur was followed by King Henry II.

READING CHALLENGE

After reading "King Arthur," answer the following questions.

1. **Arthur was a legendary _____ from the Middle Ages.**
   A. knight   B. magician   C. king   D. prophet

2. **Merlin was a _____.**
   A. king   B. knight   C. magician   D. hero

3. **Arthur married the beautiful_____.**
   A. Lady of the Lake   B. queen   C. Guinevere   D. princess

4. **Arthur was the only person in the kingdom who was able to _____.**
   A. fight and win his battles
   B. prepare his kingdom for fighting
   C. pull the sword out of the stone
   D. have a knight to be in charge of the court

5. **The reign of King Arthur is said to have been followed by _____.**
   A. King Edward   B. King James   C. King Henry II   D. no one

6. **The tradition of King Arthur's knights was to sit at this type of table.**
   A. rectangle   B. round   C. square   D. oval

*Total Correct*_____   23

President Abraham Lincoln

Abraham Lincoln was the sixteenth president of the United States and one of the most famous. He made many great contributions to our nation in the time of his presidency. Growing up in Indiana as a young boy, Lincoln took the opportunity to learn very seriously. He was an excellent student. He went to school during the day, helped his family with chores in the afternoon and studied feverishly at night. His studying was done by candlelight.

Lincoln grew up to be a serious student as a young adult too. He became a lawyer and felt strongly about being honest and having personal integrity. He became known as "Honest Abe," because of the high moral standards he set for himself.

Mr. Lincoln was very active in state politics, and later, in congress. He became unpopular for a while because he did not believe in slavery. After being away from congress and state politics for some time, the attitude toward slavery changed across the nation. Mr. Lincoln then regained his popularity with the American people.

In 1861, he was elected to the highest office in our country, President of the United States.

READING CHALLENGE

After reading "Mr. Lincoln," answer the following questions.

1. **Abraham Lincoln had an early career as a:**
   A. doctor.   B. banker.   C. lawyer.   D. scientist.

2. **How did Abraham Lincoln feel about school?**
   A. He took it very seriously.   B. He didn't like it very much.
   C. He felt like it made him study too much.   D. He wished he didn't have it.

3. **What were his earlier jobs in politics?**
   A. He was a congressman.
   B. He was a senator.
   C. He was a governor.
   D. He was a state legislator and congressman.

4. **Why was Lincoln unpopular for a while?**
   A. He was against slavery in the United States.
   B. He didn't agree with the trade rules with Indians.
   C. He wanted to start a war.
   D. He felt that some people were not as honest as he was.

5. **Abraham Lincoln was the _____ U. S. President.**
   A. 14th   B. 15th   C. 16th   D. 17th

*Total Correct*_____

THE CROSSWORD CHALLENGE
President Abraham Lincoln Puzzle

ACROSS

1. Comes after fifteenth.
4. Very well known.
6. People called him "_____ Abe."
9. This means "being well liked."
10. He grew up in a log_____.
11. The leader of our country.
13. He had a career as this before he became President.
14. How our country chooses a leader.

DOWN

2. Lincoln's home state.
3. Not short.
5. One who attends school.
7. He was against this southern custom.
8. The light from this helped Abe study at **night**.
12. A synonym for intelligent.

Total Correct_____

Libraries

Books are not the only things you can find in libraries. Today, libraries offer many types of services, as well as materials. All types of people use libraries too. Some colleges and universities have divided their libraries into different rooms or buildings to better organize their materials. Some of the areas are medicine, religion, and law.

Local governments have budgets to support libraries in communities. Often parents can take their children there to find information for a school assignment or just to read for pleasure.

Adults also use public, community libraries. Information that has been collected over the years and new material are often helpful to business people. Libraries can help them by loaning their books, and magazines, and by allowing them to use their computers.

People who work in libraries are generally called librarians. There are many departments in libraries, making it necessary to have special librarians. For example, in the reference section you find the reference librarian. This person can assist visitors in their work and make it easier to efficiently locate the information they need.

READING CHALLENGE

After reading "Libraries," answer the following questions.

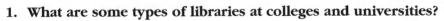

1. **What are some types of libraries at colleges and universities?**
   A. law, public and medical
   B. political, law and children
   C. law, religion and medicine
   D. book, magazine and computer

2. **Why would a person need to use a library?**
   A. reading, looking for information, use computers
   B. reading, eating, making a model
   C. talking, playing, going to college
   D. attending sports events, taking a trip

3. **Why do libraries have specialized librarians?**
   A. to help buy new books faster
   B. to help people locate their information efficiently
   C. to help make people read more books
   D. to help people remember to be quiet

Think about your local school or community library. Make a list of the things you can do there and share it with a parent or friend. Plan a trip to your library for fun!

Total Correct _____

Computers

People in our world are using computers more and more every day. Computers are being used in banks, restaurants, schools, offices buildings, telephone companies and thousands of other places. Computers are very helpful machines, but they are not able to reason and think like people. We have to tell the computers what they need to know. Sometimes the engineers who work on computers, called computer programmers, may be creating a computer to add numbers. If the programmer inputs the wrong information, the computer will not know it is wrong. Computer programming is a very important job. These trained people have to understand everything about how the computer works. They must be sure the information they install is absolutely correct. Trying out a lot of ideas to see what works and what doesn't is part of the job of a computer programmer.

Computers are designed to make work faster and easier. It is important to practice using your computer for small tasks and large ones in order to become familiar with how it works. Adults and kids can use computers effectively. Keyboarding is an important computer skill. Knowing the functions of the keys is helpful too. Computers will only become more and more popular in the future.

READING CHALLENGE

After reading "Computers," answer the following questions.

1. People use computers for the following reasons:

2. The trained people who work on computers are called:

Remember, if you don't know what a word means, look it up in a dictionary! You'll do better in the exercises!

3. Why do you think computers are becoming so popular?

4. According to the article, it is important to practice using a computer because:

THE CROSSWORD CHALLENGE
Computers Puzzle

ACROSS

4. What you hear from a computer's audio speakers.
6. Another term for the data that is stored on a computer.
8. A pointing device.

DOWN

1. The hardware item used for typing.
2. The part of the computer which contains the viewing screen.
3. The computer's storage size.
5. The software application or game running on the computer.
7. A device onto which files are copied.

Total Correct _____

28

MATH

Math is a very important subject to study. For some people, it is their favorite subject in school. Math is basically a system of working with numbers. It includes working with the relationships among numbers and operations. There are a variety of math topics that are very specific to various kinds of problems. For example, geometry involves the study of shapes, and algebra studies expressions and relations and symbols.

the fundamentals of math. From counting to working with fractions, teachers realize this is the necessary base to build on as we learn more about math.

Some people say math is like a puzzle. This is because there is often an answer to find. We approach puzzles knowing the pieces we have to work with and the missing pieces. We then take steps to find the missing pieces in a logical way. That is a good way to approach math. Math is logical and reasonable and it should be possible to imagine what you are doing when working out a problem.

Elementary school teachers may refer to math as arithmetic. This is because it describes

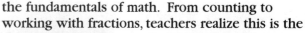

READING CHALLENGE

After reading "Math," answer the following questions.

1. **Math is a broad subject that covers areas like:**
   A. algebra, geometry, science.
   B. geometry, counting , multiplication.
   C. adding, geometry, handwriting.
   D. counting, thinking, drama.

2. **Arithmetic refers to the _____ operations of math.**
   A. harder
   B. easier
   C. fundamental
   D. unknown

3. **Finding answers to math or to a puzzle one may try to work in a reasonable or _____ way.**
   A. simple
   B. logical
   C. difficult
   D. rapid

4. **One way to help understand math and make it seem "real," is to _____ it in your mind.**
   A. remember
   B. study
   C. imagine
   D. dream

5. **People use math every day in all types of jobs and situations. Interview a parent or relative. List as many ways of using math you can think of.**

THE CROSSWORD CHALLENGE

MATH PUZZLE

ACROSS

3. Reasonable thought pattern.
4. The result in a division problem.
8. The solution to a multiplication fact.
11. The answer in a subtraction problem.

DOWN

1. A faster way of adding the same amount several times.
2. The answer in an addition problem.
5. The lowest prime number.
6. To figure by using approximate values.
7. To use math to find the answer.
9. To separate into equal amounts.
10. The lowest even number.

Total Correct _____

The Making of A Movie

Every week people go to the movies. It is certainly one of our greatest forms of entertainment. We can let our imaginations go back in time when we see a movie about a historical event. We can feel like we are in a high speed race car because of the sophisticated cameras used today. Making a movie is a very time consuming process, but, in the end, the hard work pays off.

Many different jobs are involved in the process of making a movie. The actors and actresses are obvious parts of the team because we see them on the screen. The "behind the scenes," people are often not thought of, but are certainly very important. The director is the person who starts and stops the scenes and advises the actors on how to better do their part. The camera operator, of course, does the actual filming. Often, there are several cameras used in making a movie. After the filming is done, the film editor takes the finished film and works with the director to cut and reattach the scenes together. This allows the film to roll the scenes in the correct order. The work is hard for everyone and it is important for the team working on a movie to work together and be ready when it is time for them to do their special part.

READING CHALLENGE

After reading "The Making of A Movie," answer the following questions.

1. **Movies are a form of_____ for audiences.**
   A. entertainment   B. driving   C. work   D. visiting

2. **The obvious team members on a movie crew are the:**
   A. editors and directors.
   B. actors and directors.
   C. actors and actresses.
   D. camera operators.

3. **Making a movie is an act of _____among the crew.**
   A. acting   B. teamwork   C. pretending   D. filming

4. **After the film is made there is still some work for these people:**
   A. actors and actresses.
   B. director and film editor.
   C. camera crew and make-up artists.
   D. director and audience.

5. **The phrase "behind the scenes," means:**
   A. unimportant.   B. not filmed.   C. the end.   D. backstage.

The Reading Contest

Meg decided to enter a reading contest because reading was her favorite hobby. Being in the fourth grade, she thought this would be a great way to spend her spare time over the Christmas break. The contest was held at the public library near her house. The rules were to read ten books in two weeks. Each book had to be at least one hundred pages long, and the winner would receive a new bike. Meg had selected her books and already started reading. On the last day of school, Meg asked her friend Ruth what she planned to do over the holidays. Ruth proceeded to tell her she was entering the library reading contest. Meg was shocked! Now her best friend was competing against her.

Carefully, Meg began to explain to her friend that she had also entered the contest. The girls talked about the requirements of the contest and decided to have fun and be friends even if the other one won. Soon the day was over and the girls went home for the holiday break. Meg went to her room and began sorting her books into stacks according to the order she planned to read them. Meg decided to get busy so she picked up a book she had already started reading, lay on her bed and read. She finished the book an hour later and was thrilled with the story.

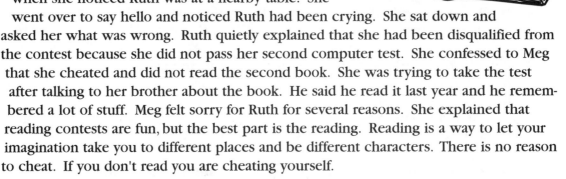

The next day Meg entered the library to take the computer quiz on the book. This score would tell the contest judge if she really had read the book. Meg felt the quiz was easy and was preparing to leave when she noticed Ruth was at a nearby table. She went over to say hello and noticed Ruth had been crying. She sat down and asked her what was wrong. Ruth quietly explained that she had been disqualified from the contest because she did not pass her second computer test. She confessed to Meg that she cheated and did not read the second book. She was trying to take the test after talking to her brother about the book. He said he read it last year and he remembered a lot of stuff. Meg felt sorry for Ruth for several reasons. She explained that reading contests are fun, but the best part is the reading. Reading is a way to let your imagination take you to different places and be different characters. There is no reason to cheat. If you don't read you are cheating yourself.

Ruth thought about the things Meg said and decided that she was right. She felt horrible about being dishonest and decided to read all of the books for the contest anyway. That way she and Meg could talk about the stories together just like they did at school when they read in class. This really was a good lesson for Ruth. She was impressed by the approach Meg took for the contest. Meg had entered the contest simply because she just liked reading! The prize was not the real reason for being in the contest. Ruth decided that was the best attitude to have and next time she would try that too.

READING CHALLENGE

After reading "The Reading Contest," answer the following questions.

1. **The rules for the contest were:**
   A. read 100 books in 2 weeks.
   C. read 10 books in 2 weeks.
   B. read 10 books in 10 weeks.
   D. read 2 books in 100 days.

2. **The girls were in the _____ grade.**
   A. 3rd   B. 5th   C. 4th   D. 6th

3. **The contest was taking place over the:**
   A. summer.   B. Christmas break.   C. weekend.   D. year.

4. **Why was Meg taking a test on the computer?**
   A. Because the judge told her to try it.
   B. Because her score would prove she read the book.
   C. Because Ruth did not pass it.
   D. Because the winner had taken it last year.

5. **What were Meg's reasons for reading?**
   A. She wanted to win the bike.
   B. She liked reading and using her imagination.
   C. She wanted to beat Ruth.
   D. She was doing a project.

6. **In your own words, explain how Ruth changed from the beginning of the story to the end. Include influences you remember from the story that you think caused her to change. Use a separate sheet of paper for your answer.**

Remember, if you don't know what a word means, look it up in a dictionary! You'll do better in the exercises!

ROCK HOUNDS

Ann was going to the garage to get her bike for an afternoon ride when she discovered a shiny rock on the ground. She picked it up and examined it closely, turning it over and over. The rock was black with smooth surfaces and a few sharp edges. Ann forgot about her bike ride and took her treasure inside to show her mother. Ann asked if she had seen anything like it before. Her mother thought that she had, but wasn't exactly sure.

Ann's father came into the room. He looked at the stone and explained that he once had a rock like this in a collection. It was called obsidian and it was used by the Indians to make arrowheads. Ann was very interested by this information. She questioned her father as fast as she could about this rock collection. She wanted a rock collection herself now.

"I had no idea rocks could be so interesting. There must be millions," she said.

"Yes there are. I should have kept up this hobby. I had just a small collection, about thirty rocks," replied Ann's father.

"Sounds like you enjoyed it." Ann said.

"Yeah, I was just a 'rock hound' back then," he laughed.

"You were a what?" Ann asked.

"A rock hound. It's a person who has a hobby of collecting rocks," her father explained. "I suppose it is a rather odd nickname."

"That's a funny name for a rock collector. I don't know if I want to be called a rock hound, but I still think I'd really like this hobby. It seems interesting. I could find out where rocks come from and how they develop too," Ann predicted.

"Oh yes. In fact, rocks are formed by processes in the earth. Some are results of high temperatures. Others are products of immense pressure in the earth. And the sedimentary types are collections of layers of materials," her father explained.

"I think I'll begin today just looking around the neighborhood. Surely I can find some rocks here. You can join me Dad. Will you?" Ann asked.

"Sure," her dad replied.

READING CHALLENGE

After reading "Rock Hounds," answer the following questions.

1. **What did Ann do first?**
   A. go inside   B. ride her bike   C. find a stone   D. watch T.V

2. **What is the nickname of a rock collector?**
   A. gadget   B. rock hound   C. rockie   D. hardhead

3. **Why did her father know so much about rocks?**
   A. Because he is a teacher.   B. Because he was trying to impress her.
   C. Because he was a rock hound.   D. Because his school was in the Rockies.

4. **Where does Ann decide to go look for rocks?**
   A. the mountains   B. the playground
   C. her backyard   D. the neighborhood

5. **What does the phrase "formed by earthly processes," mean?**
   A. The earth makes everything.   B. Earth's conditions can form rocks.
   C. Earthquakes are bad for rocks.   D. All rocks grow in the earth.

6. **How did Ann's father know about the Indians using the obsidian stone for making arrowheads?**
   A. He studied about it when he was younger.
   B. He is an Indian.
   C. He likes to play Indian games.
   D. He wants Ann to be smarter about rock collecting.

7. **In the space provided, list five steps Ann could follow to make a rock collection for herself.**

THE CROSSWORD CHALLENGE

ROCK HOUNDS PUZZLE

ACROSS

3. An old Indian tool.
9. A rock form that is made from a collection of material settling down.
10. The planet we call home.

DOWN

1. Warmth.
2. Weight that is applied on some types of rocks.
4. A fun pastime.
5. One who collects.
6. Not rough.
7. A polished looking reflection.
8. Levels of the Earth.

Total Correct _____

RBP

John's soccer team was called the Riverdale Patriots. He was captain of the team last year and he hoped to captain one more year before he left middle school. Sam, John's best friend, was co-captain. They had a great record last year. Hopefully this year would be as successful. Soccer was important to both of them, but they knew that working together on a team was most important.

One day Sam called John and told him something was up. He went on to explain that Mr. Stevens, their coach, was not going to be able to coach the team any more. John could not believe the news. Sam told John that Mr. Stevens had been promoted with his company and he would be traveling a lot during the soccer season. He felt this erratic schedule would be unfair to the team.

This really disappointed the boys. But, they went on discussing the problem this made for the Patriots. They tried thinking of other players that had dads who knew soccer. Finally, John suggested calling Andy's uncle. Mr. Barber was Andy's uncle. He was a huge fan, and was always at the Patriot's games. He even played soccer in college.

"You know, this is just a volunteer kind of job. We certainly can't be angry with Mr. Stevens," said John. "He was a great coach and it will be tough to do a season without Coach Stevens, but we should respect his need to stop coaching."

"Yeah, it's his company job that matters most. We know he'll always remember the Riverdale Patriots," said Sam. "In fact, whenever he is in town, he will probably come to our games."

"Yeah, you're right. I hope he does. Okay, then let's call the community recreation department and tell them about our idea of asking Mr. Barber to help out the Patriots. They may have already spoken to some people about taking the job, but we can still call. Maybe they didn't think of Mr. Barber," John said.

The boys headed for Sam's house to call the center to offer their suggestion. Sam's mom was working on dinner in the kitchen when the boys arrived. They explained their problem to Mrs. Sanders and tried calling the community recreation department. The secretary said the team had been assigned a new coach. The new coach of the Riverdale Patriots will be Jim Barber. Elated, the boys cheered and started jumping in the air, slapping hands and shouting.

READING CHALLENGE

After reading "The Patriots," answer the following questions.

Respond to each statement by writing "T," for true and "F," for false.

1. _____ Sam and John had been on different soccer teams last year.

2. _____ Mr. Stevens would not be their coach this year.

3. _____ Andy's uncle was Jim Barber.

4. _____ Mr. Stevens' job involved a lot of travel.

5. _____ The team was operated by the community boys club.

In your own words, answer the following questions in the space provided.

6. **Explain why you think the boys wanted to find a new coach for their team.**

7. **From the information given in the story, how do you think the boys felt about Mr. Stevens after they heard the news?**

8. **Perhaps you have been a part of a team or group that has experienced changes. How did the changes make you feel? Talk about this with a friend or a parent.**

Total Correct _____

Jenny's Vacation

As soon as school was out in June, Jenny and her family were leaving on vacation. Jenny was very excited because her friend Leslie was able to come along. Jenny's family had planned this trip out West for a long time. Living in South Carolina, Jenny felt that Colorado, Nevada and Arizona seemed a long way off. Jenny's father had graduated from the University of Arizona about twenty years ago when he was twenty-one. Now he was going to show his family his college and the beautiful state of Arizona.

Jenny was preparing a list of things she wanted to do and see once she arrived in each state. She had lots of film in her camera and she insisted Leslie bring a camera too. The next year in school Jenny and Leslie would be in the fourth grade. They could do an awesome report on these states when they had first hand knowledge of the subject. The time finally came for the Jacobs family to leave. The car was loaded with suitcases and hiking gear and a picnic basket full of snacks was placed in the back seat. Leslie and Jenny hopped in the car and Mr. Jacobs started up the car. Suddenly, Jenny remembered Toby, the family dog. "Oh no, Mom, what about Toby?" she exclaimed.

"I thought you might finally remember poor Toby," her mom answered. "I have made arrangements for him to stay at the Hendersons' while we are gone. Mr. and Mrs. Henderson said they would be glad to keep Toby for us. After all, he is a veterinarian, so we know Toby is in good hands."

"Wow, that's great. Sam, the Hendersons' son, likes Toby a lot. That's perfect!" said Jenny. "Boy, I was so involved with this trip I forgot about one of my best friends."

"Are we ready to go now?" asked Mr. Jacobs.

"Yes, we're ready. I can't think of anything else I have forgotten," said Jenny. The Jacobs pulled out of their driveway, leaving their home behind and ready to embark on their westward journey.

READING CHALLENGE

After reading "Jenny's Vacation," answer the following questions.

1. **What states were Jenny and her family planning to visit on their trip?**
   A. Nevada, Texas and Arizona
   B. Nevada, Arizona and Colorado
   C. Oklahoma, Colorado and Arizona
   D. Tucson, Nevada and California

2. **When were the Jacobs planning to leave for their vacation?**
   A. after her father came in from work
   B. before her birthday
   C. as soon as school was out in June
   D. after the game

3. **Why was the family going to visit a college in Arizona?**
   A. because she may want to go there
   B. to see the tall buildings
   C. because her father attended there
   D. to take some pictures

4. **Leslie was supposed to bring along her own. . .**
   A. camera.
   B. backpack.
   C. music.
   D. swimsuit.

5. **Who is Toby?**
   A. the Jacob's next door neighbor
   B. the family dog
   C. a co-worker of Mr. Jacobs
   D. the veterinarian

6. **Why was Toby going to be with the Hendersons?**
   A. because he was sick
   B. because they agreed to pet-sit
   C. because they found him
   D. because they liked him

7. **Which word means about the same as "embark?"**
   A. attempt
   B. survive
   C. begin
   D. chop

8. **Which word means about the same as "first hand?"**
   A. conceal
   B. without
   C. primary
   D. last

9. **Which word means about the same as "gear?"**
   A. equipment
   B. stages
   C. foods
   D. humor

Remember, if you don't know what a word means, look it up in a dictionary! You'll do better in the exercises!

THE CROSSWORD CHALLENGE

Jenny's Vacation Puzzle

ACROSS

3. A token to remember a place by.
6. Mail you might send to a friend while you are gone.
7. A fancy place to stay on a vacation.
8. Luggage.
12. A device for taking photos.
13. A fast way to travel.

DOWN

1. A common pasttime for travelers.
2. A warm season for people to take vacation.
4. A visitor to a new place, one taking a tour.
5. A popular hot, sandy vacation destination.
9. A popular summer, water activity.
10. To put everything into a suitcase, preparing for a trip.
11. To go places.

*Total Correct*_____

The Ballet Swan

Maria was very mad when her mom picked her up from ballet class. Her face was all wrinkled up and her arms were folded across her chest.

"What's wrong?" her mother asked. Maria got in the car, slammed the door, and yelled, "Swans!"

"Swans?" her mother questioned.

"Yes, Swans. Every year I have to be a stupid swan in the ballet. I want to be something else — anything else — not just a swan. Lisa always gets different parts each year. I know she's not that great. I don't know why I never get anything different," Maria fussed.

"Well, Maria, first you need to calm down and think about what being a swan involves. I'm sure Mrs. Dupree has her reasons for casting you as a swan," her mother said.

"Well, I can't imagine why," scoffed Maria.

Just as Maria and her mom prepared to leave the parking lot, Mrs. Dupree came out of the ballet studio waving her hands. She obviously wanted them to wait so she could speak to either Maria or her mother. Maria rolled down the car window to hear what she wanted to say. Mrs. Dupree came over to the car and handed Maria a bag.

"Here is the headpiece to your swan costume, Maria. Mrs. Coleman, did Maria tell you about her role as the lead swan this year? She'll be on stage throughout the entire ballet. I'm so proud of her progress. She's quite a dancer," said Mrs. Dupree.

"Well..I..I..did tell her I was a swan," said Maria. "I guess I didn't realize I was the lead this year. Sorry I forgot my headpiece."

"That's fine, you go on now and rest. You had a great performance today. Hey, thanks for being my number one swan," said Mrs. Dupree.

Mrs. Dupree walked away and Maria turned to her mom and smiled. Her mom smiled back and said, "Gee, the lead swan, huh? That's pretty good Maria."

They both laughed and rode home smiling about the misunderstanding.

READING CHALLENGE

After reading "The Ballet Swan," answer the following questions.

1. **Why was Maria so mad about being a swan?**
   A. because she didn't like the costume
   B. because she was not with her friends
   C. because she had always been one
   D. because she wanted to be the girl

2. **What was Mrs. Dupree's reason for choosing Maria to be a swan?**
   A. because she was tall
   B. because she liked her
   C. because she already knew how
   D. because she was a good dancer

3. **Why was this year's swan role so important for the performance and Maria?**
   A. because it was the last
   B. because her dad would be watching
   C. because it was the lead role
   D. because she would do her best

4. **Why did Mrs. Dupree come out to the Coleman's car?**
   A. to tell Maria to practice   B. to give her a treat
   C. to bring the headpiece   D. to tell her not to practice

5. **In your own words, tell how you think Maria felt after Mrs. Dupree told her she was her number one swan.**

Think of a situation you may have been in before that had you confused. What did you do to figure it out? Did it seem "not so bad" once you got all of the facts? Discuss this with a parent. Find out their ways of handling a confusing situation.

Spirit in Baseball

Sam had always wanted to be on the baseball team at his school. Finally, this year he made it! The coach assigned him to center field and put him fifth in the batting order. Preparing for his first game was exciting. Sam got to the locker room early. He dressed out in his fresh new red and white uniform and admired himself for a minute in the mirror. Soon, other teammates arrived. The boys began helping their coach gather the equipment they would need for the game. Sam had been so excited all day he was finding it hard to stay calm. He was also forgetting things. He even forgot to eat his dinner.

The team was all ready. Time for the game was close. The players headed for the diamond. Sam couldn't have been more proud. The game started and Sam's team was on fire! Sam was in center field. He caught four out of five fly balls in the first inning. He was really doing a great job. What a great baseball debut!

He soon got a chance at bat. He knocked two balls to center field. He batted one runner in and helped two others advance bases. The innings went by quickly. After the last pitch of the game was thrown, a fellow teammate knocked it over the wall for a nine-to-seven victory. Sam, his team and the coach went wild! They won! What a game! Sam had played his first baseball game and won. What a wonderful feeling.

The team started for the locker room when Sam heard a small voice. Sam turned and saw his little neighbor, Kevin.

"Hey, Sam, I hope I can play as good as you when I get to be big," said Kevin.

"Oh, Kevin, I am sure you will be. You just have to want to do it real bad," replied Sam. Kevin smiled, and waved and turned to go join his father. Sam felt good knowing Kevin was watching him. He had watched older boys too. Sam hoped this game and this night would stay in Kevin's mind. Then one day he could be like Sam and see a dream come true. Sam knew what a great game baseball can be and it looked like Kevin was catching on too.

READING CHALLENGE

After reading "Spirit In Baseball," answer the following questions.

1. **What is the meaning of the word <u>diamond</u> as it is used in the story?**
   A. ring   B. field   C. stone   D. glass

2. **What does the author mean by the phrase "Sam's team was on fire?"**
   A. The team was doing great.
   B. The dugout was a fire.
   C. A fan started a fire.
   D. The team was dressed in red.

3. **What is meant by the term "debut" in the story?**
   A. a first time playing baseball
   B. a game that is important to win
   C. a way to play the game
   D. a sure way to win

4. **Why was Sam so excited about the baseball game?**
   A. Because it was his first time playing first base.
   B. Because he finally got to play on the high school team.
   C. Because he had his friend Kevin watching him.
   D. Because he was good at baseball and wanted to show everyone.

5. **What was the reason for Kevin's remark to Sam at the end of the game?**
   A. Kevin and Sam usually talk after a game.
   B. Sam wanted Kevin to get him a drink.
   C. Sam and Kevin were brothers.
   D. Kevin was admiring Sam and wanted to get his attention.

6. **How did Sam treat Kevin when he spoke to him after the game?**
   A. He was kind.   B. He was rude.
   C. He didn't notice him.   D. He laughed at him.

7. **In your own words, explain why little kids often "look up to" or admire older kids.**

THE CROSSWORD CHALLENGE

Spirit in Baseball Puzzle

ACROSS

1. What a baseball field is called.
3. Equipment for hitting the ball.
5. Protective hand gear for catching balls.
6. A hit that allows the runner to run all bases and score.
8. The player who throws the batter the balls.
11. Person hitting the ball.

DOWN

2. Three of these per team, per inning.
3. Locations the runner goes to.
4. The team's leader.
7. The "judge" in the game.
9. A score.
10. People who came to the game to cheer.

Total Correct _____

RBP

46

VISITORS

All along the path
I watched where the flowers were blooming.
It seemed unfair that soon Mother Nature
would rob them of their color and health.

Seasons stop by to visit.
Relatives come in for Thanksgiving and Easter.
They move on and we forget
the cool air and warm sunshine.

If only we could appreciate the time they are here.
We might be tolerant of the extremes.
Because they will soon be gone
and the conditions will be reversed.

Summer, winter
fall, spring
aunt, uncle
grandparents too
all we have is to enjoy.

47

READING CHALLENGE

After reading "Visitors," answer the following questions.

1. **What two things is the author comparing in the poem?**
   A. seasons and weather
   B. relatives and seasons
   C. months and people
   D. climate and time

2. **Why are the flowers going to be "robbed," of their health?**
   A. most plants don't live long
   B. flowers are not good plants
   C. the harsh cold will kill them
   D. someone will pick them

3. **How did the author compare the seasons to people in the second stanza?**
   A. by associating the seasons with the temperatures
   B. by stating that both are visitors stopping by
   C. by comparing the holidays
   D. by stating that people forget things

4. **In your own words, how are we to appreciate the things the author compares in the fourth stanza?**

5. **What do you think the author's purpose is in writing this poem?**

Total Correct _____

Ski School

Billy's family was leaving for their family vacation in one week. He was less than thrilled about it. As usual, they were going to Utah to ski. They do this every year. The Dansen family goes to the same ski lodge, the same restaurants, the same ski school every year. This year would be no different. It would be okay if only Billy wasn't leaving for vacation at the same time his best friend, Jason, would be moving.

Billy and Jason had been in school together since kindergarten. This was their first year at middle school. Sixth grade was much easier to handle with your best friend by your side. Billy reluctantly filled out his registration for ski school lessons and gave it to his mom. He even got all of his ski equipment and clothes together before he had to listen to her fuss about running late. He hoped his attitude would get better. He did, at least, have another week to hang out with Jason. It would be really weird to not have Jason around anymore.

The week passed much too quickly and the Dansens left for Utah. They arrived at their hotel and unpacked. Mr. Dansen went over the schedule of activities for the week. After it was read aloud it seemed terribly confusing. Then Mr. Dansen explained that everyone must be responsible for his own ski school times and keep up with their tickets for the lifts. Billy would begin class early in the morning, so he gathered his things and prepared for a busy day on the slopes. After dinner, everyone headed to bed. It had been a long day. Billy couldn't help lying in bed thinking about Jason and his family leaving their comfortable home with the huge backyard. He and Jason had some great times in that yard. Finally he went to sleep, convincing himself that this is part of growing up.

Sometimes we can't help changes that occur.

As Billy got to his slope location for his first day with the instructor, he had not overcome his frustration of being on this vacation during Jason's move. He slowly trudged up to the crowd of anxious skiers and tried to hear the muffled voices of the ski team instructors. Billy wasn't really paying attention to the announcements. He was too distracted by his thoughts. Suddenly, he heard a familiar voice. He jerked around to see where it was coming from and there, wrapped in a blue ski suit with red gloves and a silly hat, stood Jason.

"Hey, Jason, what are you doing here?" Billy exclaimed.

"I'm attending my first day at ski school," replied Jason.

"But...but..your...move," Billy stammered.

"Yeah, we were going to move, but at the last minute Dad chose to go to a different department in his company. He said that would be better for his family," Jason explained.

"Wow, I knew your dad was a smart guy, but I never dreamed..," Billy started.

"Well, I think this was probably his smartest decision so far. I was not at all happy about moving, but I know my dad thinks things through before he does anything. Especially anything huge like a move," Jason said.

"Yeah, I was hating this whole vacation because I wasn't even going to get a chance to say good-bye to you. I had to leave on this stupid trip," said Billy.

"Well, now you can say good-bye, or I guess maybe 'hello'," laughed Jason.

Ski School (continued)

"This is awesome! I guess sometimes you never know how things will turn out. I am so glad you aren't moving. And it's awesome that you're here! I guess we better go find out what we'll be doing today," said Billy.

"Maybe we are in the same group. I sure hope so," Jason said.

The boys headed for the instructors to get their schedules. On the way, Billy talked about how his parents would not believe this news. He decided that maybe this vacation isn't all that bad after all.

READING CHALLENGE

After reading "Ski School," answer the following questions.

1. **What did Billy not want to do?**
   A. move with Jason
   B. get ready for the trip
   C. take a lesson
   D. try out for ski school

2. **Why was Jason's family moving?**
   A. Because Jason needed new friends
   B. Because Jason and Sam were going to ski school
   C. Because Jason's dad was being transferred
   D. Because they sold their house and had to move

3. **Where did the Dansen family go for their vacation?**
   A. a ski lodge
   B. a beach
   C. Europe
   D. a cruise

4. **What was the unexpected surprise Billy got on his first day at ski school?**
   A. The work was harder this year.
   B. The instructors were all new this time.
   C. Jason was there for ski school.
   D. Jason's dad was a ski instructor.

5. **How do you think Billy felt about the vacation at the end of the story?**
   A. He was still upset that he had to go with his family.
   B. He thought it was going to be an okay. vacation after all.
   C. He liked it, but wished his brother was there too.
   D. He was okay about the trip, but hated skiing.

Have you ever had to stick to plans that were made and something else came up that conflicted with those plans? Tell about your experience.

THE CROSSWORD CHALLENGE

Ski School Puzzle

ACROSS

1. An incline.
3. A transportation device for getting to the mountain top.
5. Teacher.
7. Hand warming clothing.
10. Place for organized instruction.
11. Apparatus worn on the feet for sliding through snow.

DOWN

1. Fluffy frozen rain, weather condition.
2. Hand held devices for pushing through snow.
4. Tall shoes.
6. Protective eyewear.
8. Face covering.
9. Weather suitable for snow.

Total Correct _____

Grayson's family had recently opened an ice cream shop. His dad had done this in two other towns before Grayson was born. This time Grayson was old enough to see the whole process of opening a store.

Each day after school Grayson asked his dad about the shop. He knew his father believed ice cream shops should be fun, cheerful places for families to go. This new shop was exactly that. The shiny white ice cream freezers were always spotless. The tables and chairs were white with red designs. The wallpaper pattern was a series of happy clowns eating ice cream. Even the menu board was lighted and had pictures of ice cream cones that were illuminated to make them look real.

Sometimes Grayson's family would go to the shop to greet customers and check on business. Grayson would sample the ice cream flavors while his parents were speaking to the customers in the shop. Everyone always seemed to be happily enjoying their ice cream treats.

On one particular evening visit, Grayson saw his soccer coach having a banana split. He couldn't believe it. It really was Coach Kern! He ran over to say "hi."

"Hey, Coach Kern!" Grayson said.

"Hey, Grayson, you're here. My son Trey said you are here sometimes. How's it going being the most popular ice cream shop in town?" asked Coach Kern.

"Well, it is great right now. We're glad everyone likes ice cream so much," said Grayson. "You know Coach, we are actually the only ice cream shop in town."

"Yeah, but that's good. You don't want too much competition. I have to tell you I just had the best banana split! But, I better go now, it was great seeing you," said Coach Kern.

"I'll tell my dad you came by. Come back soon," Grayson said.

"I sure will," replied the coach.

The coach left and Grayson went back to find his father to share the news. This was really great that even his coach had come in. Grayson beamed with pride as he was looking to find his father.

READING CHALLENGE

After reading "The Ice Cream Shop," answer the following questions.

1. **What did Grayson's father believe ice cream shops should be like?**
   A. small and quiet
   B. colorful and cheerful
   C. dimly lit and busy
   D. crowded and noisy

2. **Why was Grayson excited about visiting the shop?**
   A. to get an ice cream
   B. to see his father
   C. to work at the shop
   D. to be involved

3. **What is the reason for the family to go "check on business?"**
   A. to see if very many people are there, and if they are happy
   B. to see if the shop is open
   C. to see if the banana splits are good
   D. to let Grayson work awhile

4. **Why do you think Grayson was happy to see his soccer coach?**
   A. because he likes ice cream
   B. because he told him he wanted to practice
   C. because he was proud Coach was visiting his dad's shop
   D. because he was hoping to play more soccer this year

5. **In the space provided below, write the directions for making the best ice cream treat you can think of. Be sure to put the steps in the correct order.**

Remember, if you don't know what a word means, look it up in a dictionary! You'll do better in the exercises!

Total Correct _____

THE CROSSWORD CHALLENGE
The Ice Cream Shop Puzzle

ACROSS

1. Varieties ice cream comes in.
3. The food group ice cream is in.
7. A popular flavor of ice cream, brown in color.
8. The edible ice cream holder.
9. A thick drink made from ice cream and other ingredients.
10. What heat will cause ice cream to do.

DOWN

2. A popular flavor of ice cream, white in color.
4. The cold state best for keeping ice cream.
5. One serving of ice cream.
6. A snack after dinner.

*Total Correct*_____

Kelly's Lesson

Kelly could not wait for the summer to be over. She was going to be in the fifth grade. That meant that she could be in the school band. Being in the school band had been a dream of hers for a long time. She loved watching her older sister in parades and at football game performances. Soon she would be a part of that. Maybe one day some elementary school student would see her and want to be in the band too.

Kelly had chosen the flute as her instrument and her mother thought it would be good for her to get a few lessons. So she signed Kelly up for lessons at the local community college. Mrs. Dennis, Kelly's mother, thought this would at least help her learn to read music and get started on the basics of flute playing. Kelly was very excited about this opportunity.

It came time for her first lesson, and Kelly was both nervous and excited. She really wanted to do a good job. Her mother took her to the college fine arts building for the lesson. She parked the car and walked with Kelly to the door. Inside, they found the elevator and went to the floor of the instructor's office. Mrs. Davis, the instructor, was waiting for them. They chatted briefly and Mrs. Dennis said she would return in one hour. Kelly and Mrs. Davis went into a practice room and sat behind two large, black music stands.

Kelly saw Mrs. Davis pick up an old brownish looking flute. Kelly was surprised to see such a dirty instrument. Mrs. Davis explained that it was not really dirty, just tarnished. A good polishing would make it silver again. She told Kelly that some flutes are made of silver and others are made of nickel. She said nickel doesn't tarnish as badly as silver. Kelly had a nickel plated flute.

Mrs. Davis went over all of the basics, from holding the flute properly to blowing air into the mouthpiece. Kelly listened intently to every word. She tried to play a few notes, but it was very windy. Mrs. Davis said that was normal for beginners. She assured her she would get better. They continued to work until the lesson was over and Kelly agreed to practice. Her mom soon arrived and Kelly thanked Mrs. Davis for the lesson. Kelly was very glad she had started flute lessons. She planned her practice schedule in the car all the way home.

READING CHALLENGE

After reading "Kelly's Lesson," answer the following questions.

1. **What grade was Kelly going to be in when school began for her?**
   A. fourth
   B. fifth
   C. third
   D. sixth

2. **What was Kelly going to a college for?**
   A. summer camp
   B. a class her mom was taking
   C. a music lesson
   D. to be in the band

3. **What was the music instructor's name?**
   A. Mrs. Faulkner
   B. Mrs. Dennis
   C. Mrs. Davis
   D. Miss Kelly

4. **Why was Kelly taking music lessons?**
   A. In order to be in the band she had to take lessons.
   B. She wanted to like music better.
   C. To learn some basics about the flute.
   D. She wanted to be like her sister.

5. **Why did Kelly think her instructor had a dirty flute?**
   A. because it was tarnished
   B. because it was on the floor
   C. because it sounded funny
   D. because it was old

6. **How did Kelly feel at the end of the lesson?**
   A. She was ready to quit the band.
   B. She wanted to change instruments.
   C. She was excited and began planning her practice schedule.
   D. She wanted her mom to play the flute too.

Maggie's New House

Maggie slowly packed the items from the closet of her bedroom. She hadn't begun this awful task when her mother asked her to. So, now, she faced a deadline. Her father's new job starts in a week and Maggie's family would be moving to a new house.

Maggie liked the idea of living in a new town, but she didn't like moving into a new house. This house had been her only home. She was not interested in changing homes. Her bedroom in this house was perfect and she wished she didn't have to leave it. Mr. and Mrs. Banks, Maggie's parents, had told their daughters that the new house has a large T.V. room just for them, that all of the rooms are much bigger and that the neighborhood is great for bike riding.

Nevertheless, Maggie did not want to leave. She had started packing a few things when Candler, her sister, came into the room. The girls talked about their feelings and how they would miss the old house.

Candler began telling Maggie exciting things about the new house and Maggie listened carefully. There are some really big windows, the closets are much larger, and we will each have our own bathroom. After listening to this, Maggie confessed that she was being a little silly. The old house was very special and she would miss it, but moving on is often good too. The girls continued talking and Candler began helping Maggie pack up her things. Soon, the room looked empty. It had really lost its identifying marks. Maggie realized it was her presence and her unique decorating technique that gave the room some life. She decided the new place would be just fine. It would be all hers once she hung her posters, displayed her trophies, and arranged her stuffed animal collection.

Quickly, the girls finished the packing task and left to find their parents. They knew there would be more jobs to help do.

58

READING CHALLENGE

1. **Why was Maggie having to pack up her things in her room?**
   A. because she is getting rid of them
   B. because her family is moving
   C. because she is changing rooms with her sister
   D. because she is mad

2. **Why is Maggie's mother trying to tell her about the new house?**
   A. to help her see that it is more expensive
   B. to help her realize she will like it too
   C. to try to get her to calm down
   D. to prove to her that it is not her decision

3. **How did Candler help Maggie do her job?**
   A. She helped her pack the stuffed animals and trophies.
   B. She helped her with her homework.
   C. She helped her pack the things in her closet and bedroom.
   D. She told her when the movers arrived.

4. **After Candler and Maggie talked, how was Maggie's mood different?**
   A. She was angrier.   B. There was no change.
   C. She was more positive.   D. She was still mad at her mom.

Have you ever approached a task that you really did not want to do? Write about it below and share your thoughts with your parents or teacher. Ask them for suggestions on handling jobs that aren't what you really want to do.

Jessica's New Room

School would begin in two more weeks. Jessica had really mixed feelings about going to the fourth grade. Her older sister, Sarah, would be in the seventh grade and she had spent the entire summer warning Jessica about the dangers of fourth grade. Jessica knew that most of the warnings were just Sarah's way of teasing her, but she was still apprehensive.

One day, after looking through magazines, Jessica got an idea for giving her bedroom a new look. Her curtains had not been changed since she was in the first grade. Jessica's room was practically all pink. Even her trash can and rug were pink! She needed a more grown-up looking room. She gathered some magazines with decorating tips and marched down to her mother's basement office. She knew her mother liked well thought-out ideas and presentations, so she prepared her thoughts on the way.

She found her mother and asked for a few minutes of her time. Jessica explained that she was very excited about making great grades this year and being a top-notch fourth grader. Then she went on to say that in order for this to happen she needed a change.

Jessica placed several new magazines on a table and continued to explain that she needed to "update" her room. Her room was fine for a little kid, but she was no longer a baby. She showed some pictures of older looking bedroom styles and her mom looked at each one carefully. Jessica ended her speech and sat down, waiting anxiously for her mother's response.

Almost without a blink of an eye, her mother smiled and told her that it was a great idea. In fact, she took out a pad and pen and began making a list of things they would need to do. For almost  an hour, Jessica and her mom swapped ideas and planned her new room. They developed a plan that would take less than a month. Her mother would order some curtains and a bedspread and her father could begin painting the walls on the weekend. Jessica's father could even build her a work station in one corner of her room where she could study and store her computer.

Jessica was so excited about the change from her old room. She was sure this would make her year in fourth grade a good one.

READING CHALLENGE

After reading "Jessica's New Room," answer the following questions.

1. **How did Jessica feel about going to the fourth grade?**
   A. happy   B. scared   C. angry   D. unsure

2. **What was Sarah doing to attempt changing Jessica's feelings?**
   A. She was getting her too excited.
   B. She was making her cry.
   C. She didn't talk to Jessica about it.
   D. She was making it sound difficult and frightening.

3. **Where did Jessica first get her ideas for her new room?**
   A. magazines   B. friends   C. her mother   D. television

4. **What was the main color of her room before the change?**
   A. blue   B. yellow   C. pink   D. green

5. **Why did Jessica take the magazines to the basement?**
   A. to think about her plan   B. to show her mother
   C. to throw them away   D. to look for her father

6. **What was Jessica's father going to do for her room?**
   A. make it larger   B. paint it
   C. put in new carpet   D. paint and build a workcenter

7. **What did Jessica think of the plan she and her mother worked out?**
   A. She really liked it.   B. She thought it was dumb.
   C. She didn't care.   D. They didn't make a plan.

8. **Where could Jessica keep her computer in her "new room?"**
   A. in her closet   B. beside her bed
   C. on her work station   D. there isn't room for one

THE CROSSWORD CHALLENGE

Synonym Puzzle

ACROSS

2. Thankful.
5. Good.
6. Tote.
9. Plan.
14. Throw.
15. Smart.
16. Answer.
19. Dusk.

DOWN

1. Guide.
3. Prop.
4. Hard.
7. Fluid.
8. Lift.
10. Cuddle.

11. Attractive.
12. Talk.
13. Cool.
16. Honor.
17. Cruel.
18. Repair.

Total Correct _____

RBP

THE CROSSWORD CHALLENGE
Antonym Puzzle

ACROSS

1. Demolish.
2. Repaired.
4. Funny.
6. Blank page.
8. Stingy.
11. No pillar.
14. Polite.
15. Simple.
16. Sad.
17. Make-believe.

DOWN

1. Smooth.
3. Discrete.
5. Deep.
7. Identical.
9. Petite.
10. Slow.
12. Unfortunate.
13. True.

Total Correct _____

RBP

63

A New Puppy

Amy wanted a new puppy more than anything else. She had asked for one for her last two birthdays. Every time she brought home a good report card she asked for one. Her parents kept telling her that a puppy was a big responsibility. Amy tried very hard to convince them that she knew what a big responsiblity it was. She promised them she could do it.

However, none of these promises were getting her closer to getting that puppy. She decided to come up with a plan. Amy was going to prove to her parents that she could be a responsible pet owner. She got one of her old stuffed animals, then found an old jump rope to use for a leash. She tied the leash around the puppy's neck and practiced leading it around the house. She placed a bowl on the floor in the kitchen and pretended to give the puppy some water.

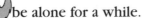

Amy pretended to have a puppy using the stuffed animal and jump rope for one week. She even took her pretend puppy outside for bathroom breaks. She was hoping this would show her parents how serious she was about wanting a real one. Everything she did was just the way she would care for a real puppy. Still, nothing worked. She decided her goal was not going to be reached. Amy put up her stuffed animal and called the plan a failure. She went to her room to be alone for a while.

Suddenly, she heard her mother calling to her. She got up and quickly went into the kitchen to see what her mother wanted. When she got to the kitchen, she saw her father standing there holding a soft tan, floppy-eared puppy. Amy was so surprised she could hardly get her words out. Her mother said that the puppy was eight weeks old and he needed a good home. Amy could not believe her eyes. This was the best thing that had ever happened to her. She had no idea her parents were going to do this. After all, her plan did work! She took the puppy gently into her arms and sat down on the floor and lovingly stroked the puppy's soft fur. Amy thanked her parents over and over while she caressed the little puppy in her arms.

READING CHALLENGE

After reading "A New Puppy," answer the following questions.

1. **When did Amy ask for a new puppy?**
   A. when she came home from school
   B. at her birthday and after her report card
   C. during her summer vacation
   D. when she talked to her mom in the kitchen

2. **Why did Amy pretend her stuffed animal was real?**
   A. She wanted to fool her friends.
   B. She was trying to frighten her cat.
   C. She was trying to show how responsible she could be.
   D. She didn't have a doll to play with.

3. **What did she use for the pretend leash?**
   A. a string   B. a ribbon   C. a belt   D. a jump rope

4. **How long did she pretend to have a dog?**
   A. a day   B. a week   C. a month   D. it didn't say

5. **Why didn't her parents want her to have a puppy?**
   A. because they are bad pets
   B. because they are big responsibilities
   C. because they are messy
   D. because they are not allowed in their house

6. **Why did her parents call her to come into the kitchen?**
   A. to clean up her mess
   B. to help prepare dinner
   C. to see her new puppy
   D. to help her mother

Remember, if you don't know what a word means, look it up in a dictionary! You'll do better in the exercises!

RBP

Sarah's Dinner

Every Tuesday night Sarah cooks dinner for her family. This particular night she could not decide what to make. She looked in the refrigerator for ideas. She saw only a few vegetables and a gallon of milk. Wondering for a while what to make, she left the kitchen to go find her older brother, Bill. Sarah found him outside shooting baskets in the driveway.

"Hey, Bill!" yelled Sarah. "What would you like for dinner tonight?"

He looked at her in a funny way and wondered if she was okay. "Sarah, you never ask me what I want for dinner. Are you sick?" he asked.

"No, I'm not sick, I just don't have any ideas. Just imagine if you were going out to eat tonight, what would you choose for dinner?" she replied.

"Oh, well, I guess I would eat at that taco place because they are giving away free pro basketball cards and you can sign up to win tickets to a game," said Bill.

"Tacos! That's it. Thanks so much Bill. You've helped a lot! Dinner will be ready soon." Sarah quickly returned to the kitchen with her idea.

The taco dinner was about to begin! Sarah knew her mother had the ingredients for tacos. She returned to the kitchen and took cheese, onions, lettuce, tomatoes, and ground beef from the refrigerator. She found her mom's frying pan and began by placing the ground beef in the pan. She placed the taco shells on the counter and started preparing the ingredients. Sarah diced the tomatoes, chopped the lettuce and grated the cheese. Her mother came in from work soon after Sarah had grated the last bit of cheese. Mrs. Moore explained to her daughter that she needed to change clothes before she began helping. Sarah continued to straighten up the kitchen and set the table for her family. Sarah's mom came in and helped her cook the beef and soon, everything was ready.

Sarah helped her mom place all of the ingredients into the taco shells. Sarah went to find her dad and her brother as her mom placed the platter of delicious tacos on the table. Soon everyone was at the table ready to eat. Even Bill was pleased with the dinner. After all it was his idea.

READING CHALLENGE

After reading "Sarah's Dinner," answer the following questions.

1. **What was Sarah looking for in the refrigerator?**
   A. the taco ingredients
   C. ideas for dinner
   B. vegetables and milk
   D. ketchup and salsa

2. **What sport did the story imply Bill is very interested in?**
   A. football   B. basketball   C. baseball   D. soccer

3. **Where was Mrs. Moore when Sarah began the dinner preparations?**
   A. at work
   C. changing clothes
   B. in the kitchen
   D. outside

4. **Why did Bill suggest tacos to Sarah?**
   A. Tacos are his favorite food.
   B. Sarah knows how to make them.
   C. He would eat tacos if he was going out to dinner.
   D. His basketball team likes tacos.

5. **How many people are in Sarah's family?**
   A. four   B. three   C. two   D. five

6. **Which best describes the ingredients Sarah prepared for the taco dinner?**
   A. beef, cheese, tomatoes, sauce
   B. cheese, tomatoes, lettuce
   C. beef, cheese, tomatoes, lettuce, taco shells
   D. beef, cheese, taco shells, tomatoes

Zoo Helpers

Melanie and Kirk went to the zoo to spend the day observing animals in natural-looking habitats. In school, they were studying about the physical and behavioral things animals do to survive. Some animals need to live in extremely cold or hot climates. Others live only in water. Some animals have to burrow underground for safety. The zoo was very interesting to Melanie as she visited the different animals' homes. Kirk wanted to see the animals in the water habitats, so they went to the zoo's huge aquarium.

After visiting the aquarium, the two friends left through the side door and saw a large pool with huge rocks in it. Playful sea lions were jumping around in the water, while others were lying on the rocks. Melanie and Kirk asked the zoo's attendant if they could feed some fish to the sea lions and he agreed. Then, Melanie heard a weak, squeaking sound, almost like a cry. She called Kirk to come listen for the sound. He heard it too. They looked all over the sea lions' pool area for the source of the sound. Finally, Kirk found something that looked odd. Melanie went over to see. There, between two rocks, was a small sea lion pup wedged underneath a large, jagged rock.

"Oh, look, I think he is stuck," said Melanie. "We need to get him some help."

"Yeah, I think he has lost his mom too," said Kirk. "You go find the zookeeper and I'll wait here."

Soon, Melanie returned with help and Kirk explained that the baby animal seemed to be running out of energy. Thankful, the zoo attendant unlocked the cage door and went in the shallow pool to gently free the stranded animal. Tired and bruised, the animal was carried away in the keeper's arms to the zoo's veterinarian.

The zoo visit was fun and certainly memorable. Melanie and Kirk felt proud of their efforts to save a helpless animal that had been unnoticed. They decided this was a great way to spend their afternoon. The zoo's manager even came to thank them for their help.

READING CHALLENGE

After reading "Zoo Helpers," answer the following questions.

1. **Where were Melanie and Kirk studying about animals?**
   A. the zoo   B. at school   C. at camp   D. at home

2. **In the first paragraph, the term "habitat," refers to:**
   A. animals.   B. water.   C. surroundings.   D. land.

3. **Which best describes the order in which their day's events occurred?**
   A. They went to the zoo, fed the animals and left.
   B. They went to the zoo, watched the animals, fed some and left.
   C. They went to the zoo, watched animals, fed sea lions and helped a pup.
   D. They went to the zoo, studied the aquarium and fed the fish.

4. **The phrase at the end of the story "running out of energy," means:**
   A. the animal was hurt and needed rest.
   B. the animal was dying and needed to be removed.
   C. the animal needed food and had been struggling for awhile.
   D. the animal was lost and scared and would soon get sick.

5. **In the space below, write about an experience you have had with an animal.
   It could be a zoo experience or one involving your own pet. Use complete sentences.**

THE CROSSWORD CHALLENGE

Zoo Helpers Puzzle

ACROSS

2. An aquatic animal with flippers for limbs.
5. An invertebrate with a hard outer shell.
6. A tropical bird.
8. A doctor specializing in animals.
10. A long-tailed animal, a primate.
12. Has black and white stripes.
14. The opposite of living in the wild, not free.

DOWN

1. A home, the natural surroundings.
3. A sea mammal, trainable.
4. A confined area for an animal.
7. Has a very long neck.
9. Large four-footed animal with a flexible trunk.
11. Having a backbone.
12. An amusement park with animals.
13. Not tame.

Total Correct _____

Christmas

The Bowers family had three children; Eleanor, Michael and Leslie. Eleanor, age twelve, was the oldest. Michael, age nine, was next and Leslie had just turned five. Every Christmas, the Bowers family would go to Memphis, Tennessee to visit their grandparents, cousins and sightsee. This year would be no different. Mr. and Mrs. Bowers always began planning this trip in the fall, after school started. By November, it was all set. The family would leave bright and early on the Wednesday before Christmas Day, arrive by noon and begin their festive visit and series of oversized meals.

Leslie, the youngest, was especially excited about going this year. She wanted to play in the large grassy field behind her grandparents' house. There was also Uncle Ted's old golf cart the older kids could drive around. Leslie enjoyed riding in the cart last year while Eleanor drove. There were horses too. Grandpa Bowers had four Tennessee Walker horses that the kids loved to ride. This was always a neat trip and this year they were excited all over again.

READING CHALLENGE

After reading "Christmas," answer the following questions.

1. **What were the Bowers going to celebrate?**
   A. Christmas   B. Thanksgiving   C. Birthdays   D. Halloween

2. **Which line below lists the three children in ages from oldest to youngest?**
   A. Michael, Leslie, Eleanor
   B. Eleanor, Leslie, Michael
   C. Eleanor, Michael, Leslie
   D. Leslie, Michael, Eleanor

3. **What were the children planning to do at their grandparents' house?**
   A. ride bikes, swim, and ride horses
   B. ride horses, ride a golf cart and play outside
   C. swim, play video games, ride to Tennessee
   D. play kickball, play golf, ride horses.

4. **How many horses does Grandpa have?**
   A. 3   B. 2   C. 1   D. 4

5. **In your own words, tell about a trip your family has taken. Perhaps your family takes a traditional trip every year to the same place. Include your favorite parts of the trip.**

RBP

The Hike

After the hike, I felt very tired. I hoped to lie down and rest.
The day was like a journey to a faraway land I didn't know.

I wanted to rest. I hoped to find energy.
My body was like a feather. The wind could blow and make me fall.

I finally saw a stream; the water was cool and kind.
I drank until I had to breathe. The water was a friend to me.

The hike was now over. I could return to civilization.
My legs were steel poles. I saw my cabin and I ran.

READING CHALLENGE

After reading "The Hike," answer the following questions.

1. **What is meant by the phrase, "my body was like a feather?"**
   A. His body was tired and weak.
   B. He was tall and thin.
   C. He was soft and the same color as the feather.
   D. He was looking at a feather he found.

2. **The author states, "I hoped to find energy." How is this possible?**
   A. He was looking for some electricity.
   B. He needed the time to rest his body and rejuvenate.
   C. He hoped to find a nurse or doctor.
   D. He wanted to spend the night.

3. **According to the poem, was the person in a city?**
   A. Yes   B. No

4. **The author uses the phrase, "my legs were steel poles." What is this?**
   A. a simile   B. a metaphor   C. a lyric   D. a verse

5. **The author writes, "the water was a friend to me." In your own words, describe what this means literally.**

Total Correct _____

Sand People

I like to draw people in the sand.
I make some tall and some are short.
Then the waves come and erase the drawings
and I get to start all over.

I use a stick to be my pencil.
And instead of paper I use the shore.
I call my museum the beach.
My patrons are the seagulls.

READING CHALLENGE

After reading "Sand People," answer the following questions.

1. **What is the author describing in the poem?**
   A. a child lying on the beach
   C. a child looking at a drawing
   B. a child drawing on the beach sand
   D. a child in a sand museum

2. **What is the artist's "eraser," according to the poem?**
   A. the waves   B. the sand   C. the stick   D. the wind

3. **What is the author comparing the stick to?**
   A. a paintbrush   B. a pencil   C. a crayon   D. a person

4. **Why does the author consider the beach a museum?**
   A. a museum often has shells
   C. artists put their work in museums
   B. a museum is like a beach
   D. museums are large like beaches

5. **A person who visits a museum is called a patron. Below, write about a time you were a museum patron. If you've never been to a museum write about how you imagine it would be.**

RBP

Valentine Cookies

It would be Valentine's Day in one week and Katie wanted to bake heart-shaped cookies with her mom. She convinced her mom to embark on the project with her. They planned to make some sugar cookies and some chocolate chip cookies. Katie always enjoyed making things in the kitchen with her mother. This time she would decorate the cookies with pink frosting and multi-colored sprinkles.

Katie and her mother agreed to do their baking project on Saturday morning. They planned to start after breakfast, since Katie had a horseback riding lesson that afternoon. She could finish the cookies and select two or three to take to the stables to her riding teacher.

Katie helped her mother prepare the dough and roll it out on the counter. Carefully, Katie pressed the cookie cutters into the dough. She then lifted the cookie cutter away and picked up the smooth heart-shaped cookie and placed it on the baking sheet. Katie worked with the heart-shaped cookie cutter for several minutes. Then she chose the square one that imprinted 'Happy Valentine's Day' on the cookie dough.

Katie and her mother baked all of the cookies and allowed them to cool. Katie began to gently pick-up the warm cookies and spread the pink frosting over the top. She finished the first tray of heart-shaped cookies and slowly added the multi-colored sprinkles on each one.

Just as Katie had finished the artistic work on each cookie, her father came in the kitchen to see the finished products. Katie offered her father a big heart cookie with frosting and sprinkles. She said he would be the very first to try her Valentine project. After the first bite, her father nodded and smiled with approval. Katie was thrilled her father liked the cookie.

The cookies were put in a large plastic container to be eaten by her family and friends. Katie and her mom cleaned up the kitchen and decided the results of their work were excellent.

It was time for Katie's riding lesson, so she went to her room to change clothes. She quickly returned to get the cookies for her instructor. Her mother was waiting for her in the car. Katie hopped in and soon left with her mom for the stables.

READING CHALLENGE

1. **What does Katie want her mom to help her do on Saturday?**
   A. ride horses
   B. have a party
   C. bake cookies
   D. go shopping

2. **Katie planned to put the following decorations on the cookies:**
   A. frosting and candy.
   B. candy and chocolate chips.
   C. frosting and sprinkles.
   D. frosting and sugar.

3. **Who sampled Katie's cookies first?**
   A. Mom
   B. Katie
   C. her brother
   D. Dad

4. **Which answer best describes the steps Katie's project followed?**
   A. cut, bake, cool, frost, sprinkle
   B. roll, bake, cut, frost, sprinkle
   C. cut, bake, frost, cool, sprinkle
   D. cut, roll, bake, cool, sprinkle

5. **Whom did Katie plan to share her cookies with?**
   A. family, friends and neighbors
   B. friends and riding instructor
   C. friends, family and riding instructor
   D. just family

Baking cookies, or any other treat, is great fun. In the space below, write about a time you have baked something for someone. How did it make you feel? Use extra paper if necessary.

Remember, if you don't know what a word means, look it up in a dictionary! You'll do better in the exercises!

RBP

Name ....

THE CROSSWORD CHALLENGE

School Things Puzzle

ACROSS

3. The score you get on your test.
6. The person in charge of the whole school.
7. One who learns.
9. Another word for exam.
11. Big and yellow, a ride to school.
12. The mid-day meal.
13. Work that is done at home.

DOWN

1. People you enjoy spending time with.
2. Physical Education, abbreviation.
4. Authors write them.
5. Material to write on, made from trees.
6. A writing instrument.
8. A special piece of furniture to sit at to work.
10. One who teaches.

Total Correct _____

Surfing the Web

Mike's family had recently bought a new computer for their home use. At school Mike, had discovered the many uses of the Internet and how helpful it can be. He constantly asked his father when they could get Internet service for their home computer. Mike's dad always said he needed to find out more before he decided to do that. Mike did not see the disadvantages of the Internet. He only saw the fun and seemingly limitless uses for it.

A few weeks passed and one day Mike arrived home from school and saw a note on the kitchen table from his father. It said, "Hello Mike. I got the service. Enjoy surfing. I'll see you tonight and we'll talk more. Love, Dad." After reading the note, Mike ran upstairs to his dad's study, sat at the computer and quickly logged on, thus activating the computer's modem. He clicked on the browser icon and waited for the modem to dial. The connection was made and he was on! He chose a web search engine and typed in "English Springer Spaniels." The computer quickly began a search and matching web sites. To Mike's surprise, he received 2,675 sites. He scrolled through the first ten and clicked on a few and read the highlights. Next, he clicked on a site and saw pictures, addresses and email listings. He read on and found four local breeders of English Springer Spaniels and printed out the page on his dad's printer.

After Mike's "surfing," he went downstairs to get a snack and soon his father came in from work. He thanked his father for agreeing to get the Internet service and quickly presented the printed pages from the web site. Mike tried to contain his excitement as he told his father about the web sites that could help them get a dog. Mike's father laughed and said he did not realize that the web would actually help Mike's pursuit of a pet. They both laughed and walked into the den to talk about the possibilities of getting a dog very soon.

READING CHALLENGE

After reading "Surfing the Web," answer the following questions.

1. **What was Mike asking his father for?**
   A. a computer   B. Internet service   C. a dog   D. a ball

2. **What was Mike's father's answer for delaying his decision?**
   A. He wanted to be sure about the cost.
   B. He wanted to be sure about the size.
   C. He wanted to get more information first.
   D. He wanted to wait until he got home from work.

3. **How did Mike find out his father had agreed to his request?**
   A. He found a note from his dad one day after school.
   B. He talked to his dad after he got home from work.
   C. He went to his father's study and worked on the computer.
   D. He called his dad to find out.

4. **The author refers to a "search" Mike did on the computer. What is this?**
   A. a way to find out if it is broken
   B. a way to locate topics on the Internet
   C. a way to look for new computer games
   D. a way to find dogs in his neighborhood

The following list of terms refers to things related to computer use.
Match each with the best definition in this context.

5. **surf**
   A. waves   B. time on the Internet
   C. using a modem   D. not given

6. **icon**
   A. pictures   B. idols   C. camera   D. not given

7. **monitor**
   A. computer   B. a topic   C. calculator   D. not given

8. **scroll**
   A. paper   B. printer   C. roll through   D. not given

9. **email**
   A. letters   B. electronic mail   C. everyday mail   D. not given

10. **site**
    A. location   B. web information   C. place to sit   D. not given

RBP

Total Correct _____

A Visit With Matisse

Henri Matisse was not planning to be an artist. He first studied law in France. Due to an illness he stopped working. He used a paint set to pass the time as his body healed. Matisse was impressed only a little by the artists of his time. He was rejected by some critics who were shocked by his bold patterns and bright colors.

Matisse was the leader of the **Fauve** movement. This was a group of French painters whose style was to use harsh brush strokes and bright colors. Fauveism was popular from about 1903 until 1907. In French, the word 'Fauve' means 'wild animal,' which is further an indication of how the style was a vivid, extreme look at nature.

Matisse painted human figures, still lifes and scenes of interiors. One school of art he attended was for textile makers. He learned the love of tapestries, fabrics and texture, which would later be seen in many of his paintings. Later in life he began to work with collages of bits of paper, cut and placed together to create an interesting composition. Matisse died at the age of eighty-three. His many travels brought him many experiences and added to and altered his career. He painted, sculpted, sketched and made his famous 'The Tree of Life' stained glass window for the Vence Chapel in France.

READING CHALLENGE

After reading "A Visit With Matisse," answer the following questions.

1. **Matisse was a famous_____.**
   A. painter   B. fabric designer   C. lawyer   D. singer

2. **The word _Fauve_ is French and it means:**
   A. harsh color.   B. squares.   C. glass.   D. wild animal.

3. **Matisse attended a school of art that taught _____design.**
   A. painting   B. textile   C. glass   D. paper

4. **The _Fauve_ movement included this style of art:**
   A. bold and bright colors and harsh brush strokes.
   B. small human figures with sad faces.
   C. still life and interior paintings.
   D. landscapes and windows of trees.

5. **Matisse died at the age of:**
   A. 38.   B. 83.   C. 78.   D. 93.

Have Some Tea

In the countries of Paraguay and Uruguay there is a popular drink called mate. It is pronounced "MA tay." The ingredients are dried leaves and shoots from a holly tree that grows in South America. The drink is made by pouring boiling water over the leaves, which soaks the flavor from the leaves. The drink has a great deal of caffeine in it and it can have a strong flavor.

In the streets of Uruguay on a cold day, many people can be seen carrying gourds which contain this beverage. A long, metal straw-like device is placed in the gourd to drink from. The holly leaves are in the gourd, and they are strained out by the metal sieve at the base of the straw.

It is very common for South Americans to offer a drink of mate to a friend when visiting. Everyone may have their own gourd or they may pass only one around for everyone to have a drink.

READING CHALLENGE

After reading "Have Some Tea," answer the following questions.

1. **What beverage do Americans have that is similar to mate?**
   A. hot tea   B. water   C. juice   D. milk

2. **What is the correct way to make the "mate," drink?**
   A. add boiling water to leaves with sugar
   B. boil leaves of a tea plant with strong spices
   C. add boiling water to holly leaves
   D. add caffeine and holly leaves together

3. **How is the beverage usually served?**
   A. in a mug   B. in a gourd   C. in a straw   D. in a kettle

4. **It is very common for what countries to offer a drink of "mate?"**
   A. US of A and Australia   B. Canada and Mexico
   C. Paraguay and Uruguay   D. England and France

5. **What keeps the leaves from going into the straw when someone is drinking it?**
   A. All of the leaves are removed after boiling.
   B. Most of the leaves are too large to swallow.
   C. The sieve at the base of the straw.
   D. There are not any leaves in the drink.

*Total Correct*_____

RBP

ART LESSONS

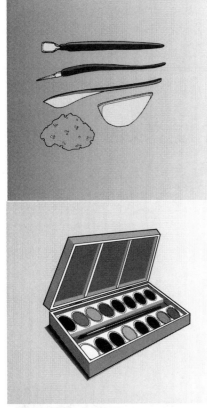

Monica had always liked her art class at school. She had even asked her mother if she could take art lessons in the summer. She thought she would have more time for this over the summer because her soccer games and music lessons would be over. Mrs. Rankin, Monica's mother, called several local teaching studios and finally found one that would be suitable for her daughter. Since Monica was a beginner, she would need to have a basic class first and then choose an area she liked the most.

On the first day of art class, Monica learned about clay and the ways to work with it, both dry and on a potter's wheel. She also saw how it is fired in a kiln to become permanently hard. She would glaze her pieces at her next class session.

The afternoon class presented watercolor painting to the students. Monica liked this very much. Her teacher, Mrs. Boykin, was an excellent watercolor artist.

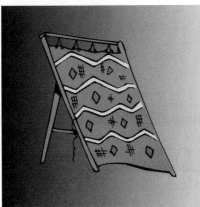

The next class session was about weaving. The studio had a huge weaving loom and everyone got a chance to practice using it. Monica chose bright colors of thread for her cloth weaving project because it would match her room. Bright colors made her happy. The other students were interested in the weaving activity too, but most of them liked the clay projects best.

Monica was very excited about the rest of the class sessions because they would be doing many different types of art.

After all of the sessions, the students were having a special event to show off their work to parents and friends. There would be rows and rows of tables loaded with art projects done by nine-year-old artists just waiting for admiring parents to see. Monica was anxiously awaiting that night.

READING CHALLENGE

After reading "Art Lessons," answer the following questions.

1. **What did Monica want to do during the summer?**
   A. play soccer   B. art lessons   C. music lessons   D. read

2. **On the first day of class, the students were introduced to _____ .**
   A. math   B. watercolor   C. clay   D. pottery

3. **How does the author describe Monica's class level?**
   A. beginner   B. advanced   C. expert   D. slow

4. **What topics did Monica's instructor cover?**
   A. clay, painting, molding, drawing
   B. clay, watercolor painting, weaving
   C. clay, basic art, water painting
   D. kiln, glaze, watercolor, weaving

5. **What was going to take place at the end of the summer?**
   A. Monica was going to be a professional artist.
   B. Monica was going to be a better musician.
   C. Monica and the class would display their work.
   D. Monica and her dad were going on a trip.

6. **Why does Monica ask her mother for art classes?**
   A. She is bad at art.
   B. She wants to learn more.
   C. She is bored.
   D. She doesn't have soccer or music in summer.

7. **Why does Monica like bright colors?**
   A. They make her cloth pretty.   B. They are easier to see.
   C. They are in her room.   D. They make her happy.

8. **Who was Monica's mother?**
   A. Mrs. Rankin   B. Mrs. Boykin
   C. Mrs. Jones   D. Not given

LONDON

London is a very large city. It is the capital of the United Kingdom of Great Britain. It is also the political center of the British Commonwealth of Nations. London is a very popular international city for trade, shopping and the arts. The country is ruled by a monarch and thus, has a rich history that continues to fascinate people everywhere. The king or queen is sometimes referred to as the sovereign leader.

Fantastic old cathedrals, theatres and parks are parts of the London we know today. Businessmen and women busily carry out their work in the City, one section of London. Another part of London is the West End. It has more of the social and entertainment aspects of London. The House of Parliament is also located in the West End.

The suburbs branch off from London in all directions. There are many attractions in the suburbs such as gardens, houses and airports. All types of transportation are available. Cars, trains, buses and an elaborate subway system called, "the Tube," are used by the people everyday. The subway trains are fast, comfortable ways to travel all over the city

Bridges provide travel from one side of the Thames River to the other. The river winds through the heart of the city in an eastward direction. Many ships import and export goods via this wide river. The London Bridge and the Tower Bridge both provide routes over the river.

A visit to London is most exciting. The history, shopping, theaters and food houses are treats. The weather is often rainy and the fog can be dense, but bad weather is not a deterrent to Londoners. It is common to see people pushing baby carriages with plastic covers shielding babies from the rain.

The city is magnificent in its ancient and modern aspects. The suburbs are equally delightful and the people are committed to the land they know as their home.

READING CHALLENGE

After reading "London," answer the following questions.

1. **London is ruled by a:**
   A. monarch.   B. king or queen.   C. sovereign.   D. leader.

2. **London is the capital of:**
   A. the United Kingdom and London.
   B. the capital of Ireland.
   C. the United Kingdom of Great Britain.
   D. the British Commonwealth of Nations.

3. **The Tower Bridge crosses this river:**
   A. the London River.   B. the Thames River.
   C. the Old River.   D. the West End River.

4. **The transportation system that is underground is called:**
   A. the river.   B. the subway.   C. the Tube.   D. not given.

5. **The Thames curves in what direction?**
   A. east   B. south   C. north   D. west

6. **London is a very popular international city for:**
   A. trade, business and people.
   B. trade, shopping and the arts.
   C. business, banks, capitals and river transportation.
   D. cathedrals, towers, bridges and Parliament.

7. **London has fantastic old:**
   A. business men and women.
   B. House of Parlament.
   C. Cathedrals, theaters, and parks.
   D. bridges.

8. **The weather in London is mostly:**
   A. sunny.
   B. rainy and foggy.
   C. snowy.
   D. cloudy.

*Total Correct*_____

Jimmy's Candy Shop Adventure

Jimmy had just turned nine and was allowed to go to the mall with his friends. It was Saturday and his friend Ron was going to meet him at the ticket booth for a two o'clock movie. The boys had done this once before and discovered the candy there is very expensive. They agreed to get some candy before the movie at a candy shop and save a few dollars that way.

Jimmy arrived at the ticket booth one hour before Ron, so he walked through the mall in search of a candy store. Jimmy was sure there was one nearby because his sister Madeline always went there. He passed a sporting goods store and saw a cool baseball jersey. It was blue and red and had the name SMOLTZ on the back. It was a copy of the one his favorite pitcher, John Smoltz, wears. Jimmy tried on the jersey and forgot all about the candy errand he was doing. He also forgot about Ron. He was thinking of only John, John Smoltz!

Moments later, he looked up and saw Ron standing in front of him, frowning. Suddenly Jimmy remembered he was supposed to be looking for the candy store. He had completely forgotten! He apologized continuously to Ron and immediately replaced the jersey. The two friends headed for the theater in hopes of getting a good seat. The scheduled time was already a few minutes past, but they hoped it was only the previews.

Jimmy felt responsible for the candy buying mess-up, so he agreed to purchase the more costly candy at the theater. He bought some chocolate covered peanuts, chewy fruit sours and sodas. The boys looked for the cinema showing the movie they were seeing and went in to find a seat. Fortunately, the day was not ruined, but the chance to save money on cheaper candy was lost.

RBP

READING CHALLENGE

After reading "Jimmy's Candy Shop Adventure," answer the following questions.

1. **Where was Jimmy planning to meet Ron?**
   A. at the ticket booth
   B. in the sporting goods store
   C. at the candy store
   D. in the mall

2. **What day of the week did the boys decide to go to the mall?**
   A. Monday   B. Saturday   C. Sunday   D. Friday

3. **What was Jimmy looking for when he went for a walk through the mall?**
   A. his sister Madeline   B. the ticket booth
   C. a candy store   D. a sporting goods store

4. **What did Jimmy find in the sporting goods store?**
   A. a baseball jersey   B. a new baseball jacket
   C. a basketball   D. candy

5. **Why was Jimmy surprised when his friend, Ron, found him in the sporting goods store? In the space below, explain your answer. Include your opinion of how Ron felt.**

Remember, if you don't know what a word means, look it up in a dictionary! You'll do better in the exercises!

Total Correct _____

RBP

ACROSS

3. A sweet, tart citrus flavor; yellow in color.
4. A sweet, fruity, chewy sugar-covered lump.
8. Like caramel, as in hard candy or sauces.
9. The most common flavor of candy canes.
10. Salt-water varieties, often it is pulled.

DOWN

1. A popular candy bar flavor; milk or dark varieties.
2. The main ingredient in most candy.
5. A nut grown in an orchard on trees.
6. A popular flavor of bubble gum; a fruit from a vine.
7. A red berry that makes a great shake.

Total Correct _____

RBP

Natalie is only eight years old and she thinks her mother treats her like she is at least fifteen. She always has to help look after her baby brother, Ryan, who is a real pest. Ryan will be four in one month and Natalie cannot seem to keep him out of her room and out of her things! All of this stuff with Ryan was really getting to Natalie when she found a great poem at school. The poem told about a girl who was going through a really hard time at her house, so she decided to find a secret place. The girl in the poem found a small door leading to the attic that was just her size. Inside she found a small spot that would be perfect. The attic floor was made of boards, and to make it comfortable, she put a small rug over them.

Natalie couldn't wait to get home and explore her house to find a secret place of her own. She even thought about looking around outside. Her secret place had to be somewhere Ryan would not find! Once she found her place, she would put a rug there too. She would even bring her box of special things she has collected and keep it there. One of her favorite things in her box was a blue necklace with a heart in the middle of it. Her grandmother gave her that when she was five.

Natalie got home and immediately began exploring.

She looked all over, both inside and out. Finally, she discovered a big tree in the corner of her back yard with big, low hanging limbs. She had never really noticed the tree before. She quickly ran over to it and climbed up to the third level of branches. She realized it was perfect for placing some boards across the branches for sitting on to think, read or just be away from Ryan.

After looking around her dad's work shed, she found the two boards she needed. She took them to the tree, placed them across the branches, took a small green rug from her bathroom and laid it on top. Carefully, Natalie climbed up to her perch. She really liked this spot. It was May and the yard was bursting with color. The tree was leafy and hid her secret spot very well. Natalie sat there for almost an hour reading her favorite book of poems. Finally, she decided to come down before her parents began to look for her. She was so glad she had a refuge, a place to go when she wanted to be alone. Her secret place was special. She skipped up the yard into the house and found her mother in the kitchen. As usual, her mother asked her to go help Ryan take a bath. But somehow this time she didn't mind so much. She knew there were times she would need to help Ryan. And now she also knew there are times she can be alone.

Natalie's Secret Place

1. **What age is the main character in the story?**
   A. 8   B. 5   C. 7   D. 4

2. **What was the girl from the poem doing in the attic?**
   A. looking for a rug   B. looking for her brother
   C. looking for a secret place   D. looking for a box from Grandmother

3. **What was Natalie's problem?**
   A. She couldn't find her brother to give him a bath.
   B. She was not finding her secret place.
   C. She had lost her blue heart necklace.
   D. She felt her mother asked her to take care of her brother too often.

4. **Where did Natalie choose to have her secret place?**
   A. her father's work shed   B. in a tree
   C. the attic   D. the bathroom

5. **Who had a rug in their secret place?**
   A. Natalie and the girl in the poem   B. Natalie
   C. the girl in the poem   D. Ryan

6. **What did Natalie plan to do in her secret place?**
   A. read   B. read, think, sleep
   C. read and play with her box   D. read, think and get away from Ryan

7. **What made Natalie's tree spot well hidden?**
   A. the beautiful May flowers   B. the leafy tree
   C. the boards   D. the green rug

8. **Why did she come down from her place after reading her poetry book?**
   A. She knew her mom was angry.
   B. She knew her dad needed the boards.
   C. It was time to bathe Ryan.
   D. Her parents would begin to look for her soon.

SCIENCE MATTERS

Matter is anything in our universe that has weight and takes up space. Matter is a way of nature showing itself to man. There are three types of matter. They are: solids, liquids and gases. They each have unique characteristics that set them apart. A solid has a definite shape, or form. It is rigid, which means it can resist most forces that can alter its shape. A liquid, however, will take the shape of the container it is in at the time. Liquids have no definite shape, but have the ability to flow. Some solids can be melted into liquids, and some liquids can be cooled or frozen to be solids. All gases have identical physical behavior. They exert pressure in all directions equally. Compared to liquids or solids, gases have lower densities. There is less matter per cubic inch in gases. Gases can be compressed or confined in a fixed amount of space.

Water is the best example of how matter looks and exists in the three different forms. If water is a liquid, it flows. It can be poured from a glass or a water hose or any other container. When frozen, it can take a definite shape in the form of ice. It depends on the container it is frozen in as to what its shape will be. In its gaseous form, water is steam. Boiling water is how water can be changed from the liquid state to the gaseous state. Scientific studies are often done on all varieties of matter. Observing, experimenting and recording data are the best ways to keep up with changes in matter in certain conditions.

Scientists realize it matters to carefully watch matter!

READING CHALLENGE

After reading "Science Matters," answer the following questions.

Directions: Decide if the items are "fact," or "opinion," based on the information in the article. Place an "F," in the blank if the statement is a fact, and an "O," if it is an opinion.

_____1. Matter has weight and takes up space.

_____2. Some forms of matter are solids, liquids or gases.

_____3. A liquid will take the shape of the container it is in.

_____4. All brown solids have the best shape or form.

_____5. Liquids are better if they are changed to solids.

_____6. Solids are easier to use.

_____7. All gases smell good.

_____8. Science is the best subject to study.

_____9. Ice tastes best when it is a round shape.

Total Correct_____

DANIEL'S HOLIDAY

Daniel had always gone to school with the kids in his neighborhood. He liked playing with Joel, David and Randy a lot. He didn't like Christmas, though. He didn't like the parties before school was out in December or anything. He didn't like it because it made him feel different. His family was Jewish and did not celebrate Christmas like his friends. His family celebrated Hanukkah.

Daniel knew all about the Festival of Lights and the eight days of Hanukkah, and of course, the gifts. He was always excited when his mom set up the menorah on the dining table. His little sister always liked making the potato latkes with their mom. It just seemed odd that his friends were not aware of these things and that he was not very well aware of Christmas.

One day Daniel told his mother about the way he felt. He asked her what he could do to make things seem more normal. She told him that it is fine to share your heritage and customs with those who have different ones. Daniel thought about this and decided she was right. He wanted his friends to experience some Hanukkah traditions and

perhaps he would experience a few Christmas celebrations.

Daniel mentioned this idea to his friends, Joel, David, and Randy. He asked them if they might be interested in coming over to his house and having some latkes and applesauce. They could see the menorah and listen to his father read some things from a Hebrew book. The boys were thrilled and they immediately accepted. The very next night, Joel's parents were decorating their Christmas tree and invited Joel's friends over for some hot cocoa and to see the tree. Mrs. Davis, Joel's mom, also had the family's Advent wreath out and they lit the very first candle. This was very special to the Davis family and Daniel saw that right away.

Each family on the street had several more holiday celebrations that year. But, thanks to Daniel, they had more variety this year than previous Decembers brought. Daniel thanked his parents for allowing him the chance to share his holiday with his friends and he was glad he experienced a little of the Christmas tradition too. Now he didn't feel quite as different.

READING CHALLENGE

After reading "Daniel's Holiday," answer the following questions.

1. **Why did Daniel feel so different from all of his friends?**
   A. because he didn't like Christmas
   B. because his family did not celebrate Christmas
   C. because his mother forgot to put up the Christmas tree
   D. because the other kids on his street weren't at his school

2. **How long does the Hanukkah Celebration last?**
   A. 5 days   B. 4 days   C. 7 days   D. 8 days

3. **What were some Jewish traditions Daniel remembers about Hanukkah?**
   A. the menorah, latkes, reading Hebrew
   B. the menorah, the lights, reading about Joel
   C. the gifts, the lights, eating potatoes
   D. the menorah, the candles, the candy

4. **How did Daniel's mother respond when he told her his problem?**
   A. She was not really listening and said things would be fine.
   B. She said it is okay to learn about other traditions.
   C. She said it was too confusing to learn another way to celebrate December.
   D. She said it was better to celebrate Hanukkah.

5. **What are some ways the Davis family celebrates Christmas?**
   A. singing, eating and tree decorating
   B. decorating the tree, lighting the Advent wreath, having hot cocoa
   C. drinking hot cocoa, lighting candles and skiing
   D. going for walks, lighting a tree, having the first lit candle

6. **Explain, in your own words, in the space below how you think Daniel felt after sharing the holidays with his good friends.**

Mile High City

One mile above sea level stands the capitol building of Denver, Colorado. Denver got its nickname "The Mile High City," from the fact that the city is exactly one mile above sea level in a particular spot. The step on the capitol building's front entrance that is exactly one mile above sea level is marked to show natives and visitors the "mile high," point. Denver is

in the western United States, and it occupies space in the northeast section of Colorado. Many people are employed by the government agencies that are located in Denver. One federal government agency there is the Denver Mint. The mint is near the capitol building and thousands of coins are made there annually.

Denver is also known for other unique treasures and facts. The air is very clear and healthy, especially for people with lung illnesses. The Rocky Mountain Region makes snow sports a huge industry for Denver. Snow ski resorts are in the suburbs of Denver and in neighboring states' cities. The winter months are very profitable for the tourist industry. After a fun day on the slopes it may be time to go have a cheeseburger. Although the hamburger was originally made in Hamburg, Germany, the first cheeseburger was made in Denver. The owner of a small drive-thru burger stand decided one day to try a slice of American cheese on the hot, juicy beef patty. From that day on, his restaurant was very busy with requests for the new 'cheeseburger.'

Denver has a number of colleges and universities as well as a school for those interested in the military. The city supports a variety of interesting opportunities for spending leisure time; everything from public libraries, to the Denver Symphony Orchestra to the professional football team, the Denver Broncos. The Broncos play their home games in Denver's "Mile High Stadium."

READING CHALLENGE

After reading "Mile High City," answer the following questions.

1. **What is the nickname of Denver, Colorado?**
   A. Snow City
   C. Mint City
   B. Mile High City
   D. Broncoville

2. **How was the hamburger changed in Denver?**
   A. It was sold in the drive-thru.
   C. A slice of cheese was added.
   B. It was made larger.
   D. More people bought them.

3. **What state is Denver the capital of?**
   A. Texas   B. Boulder   C. Colorado   D. Oklahoma

4. **What region of the United States is Denver located in?**
   A. The Northeast
   C. The Rocky Mountains
   B. The Great Lakes
   D. The Pacific States

5. **What federal agency makes coins?**
   A. the mint
   C. the university
   B. the capitol building
   D. the military

6. **What is Denver's most valuable winter industry?**
   A. tourism   B. steel   C. copper   D. cheeseburger

7. **Why is Denver called the "Mile High City?"**
   A. It is a mile from one side of the city to the other.
   B. It is a mile above sea level.
   C. It is a mile up to the top step of the capitol building.
   D. It is a mile from any other city.

8. **What reasons would a sick person have for living in Denver?**
   A. Very good doctors work there.
   B. Most medical schools there are good.
   C. The air is very clear and healthy.
   D. The food is better there.

RBP

*Total Correct*_____

Check Yourself

Page 8, Mars
1. C, 2. A, 3. B, 4. B, 5. B

Page 9, Solar System Puzzle
Across: 4. Sun, 5. Comet, 7. Moon, 9. Telescope;
Down: 1. Saturn, 2. Pluto, 3. Orbit, 6. Earth, 7. Mercury, 8. Galaxy.

Page 10, Pet Sitters Club
1. B, 2. A, 3. B, 4. C, 5. B

Page 11, Todd's Birthday
1. C, 2. B, 3. D, 4. He is proud to be given the opportunity and to share a special event with his father.

Page 12, Amazing Amphibians
1. B, 2. A, 3. C, 4. B, 5. B

Page 13, Won Ton Soup
1. China, 2. Pizza & popcorn, 3. 4, 4. The U.S. is in the Western Hemisphere.

Page 14, Keeping it Green
1. C, 2. B, 3. A, 4. D., 5. Answers will vary

Page 15, Limerick
1. C, 2. C, 3. The author seems to think it is boring, yet when studied, math is helpful.

Page 16, A Boat Ride in the Keys
1. D, 2. C, 3. C, 4. B, 5. D

Page 17, The Red Cross
1. C, 2. B, 3. A, 4. C, 5. B

Page 18, The Boys of Third Grade
1. F, 2. T, 3. F, 4. F, 5. T, 6. F, 7. F, 8. T, 9. T, 10. F

Page 19, The Airport
1. Before, 2. After, 3. After, 4. After, 5. Before, 6. Before

Page 20, Homework
1. A, 2. B, 3. C, 4. C, 5. C

Page 21, Money
1. A, 2. C, 3. B, 4. C, 5. B

Page 22, Money Puzzle
Across: 3. Bank, 4. Dollar, 6. Presidents, 8. Coins, 9. Quarter; Down: 1. Wallet, 2. Copper, 5. Dime, 6. Penny, 7. Nickel

Page 23, King Arthur
1. C, 2. C, 3. C, 4. C, 5. C, 6. B

Page 24, President Abraham Lincoln
1. C, 2. A, 3. D, 4. A, 5. C

Page 25, Mr. Lincoln Puzzle
Across: 1. Sixteenth, 4. Famous, 6. Honest, 9. Popular, 10. Cabin, 10. President, 12. Lawyer, 13. Election; Down: 2. Indiana, 3. Tall, 5. Student, 7. Slavery, 8. Candle, 11. Smart

Page 26, Libraries
1. C, 2. A, 3. B

Page 27, Computers
1. Answers will vary, 2. Programmers, 3. They do work faster, 4. Answers will vary

Page 28, Computers Puzzle
Across: 4. Sound, 6. Information, 8. Mouse; Down: 1. Keyboard, 2. Monitor, 3. Memory, 5. Program, 7. Disk

Page 29, Math
1. B, 2. C, 3. B, 4. C, 5. Answers will vary

Page 30, Math Puzzle
Across: 3. Logic, 4. Quotient, 8. Product, 11. Difference; Down: 1. Multiply, 2. Sum, 5. Two, 6. Estimate, 7. Compute, 9. Divide, 10. Zero.

Page 31, The Making of a Movie
1. A, 2. C, 3. B, 4. B, 5. B.

Page 33, The Reading Contest
1. C, 2. C, 3. B, 4. B, 5. B, 6. Answers will vary.

Page 35, Rock Hounds
1. C, 2. B, 3. C, 4. D, 5. B, 6. A, 7. Answers will vary.

Page 36, Rock Hounds Puzzle
Across: 3. Arrowhead, 9. Sedimentary, 10. Earth; Down: 1. Heat, 2. Pressure, 4. Hobby, 5. Collector, 6. Smooth, 7. Shiny, 8. Layers.

Page 38, The Patriots
1. F, 2. T, 3. T, 4. T, 5. F, 6. Answers will vary, 7. Answers will vary. 8. Answers will vary.

Page 40, Jenny's Vacation
1. B, 2. C, 3. C, 4. A, 5. B, 6. B, 7. C, 8. C, 9. A.

Page 41, Vacation Puzzle
Across: 3. Souvenir, 6. Postcard, 7. Resort, 8. Suitcase, 12. Camera, 13. Flying; Down: 1. Sightsee, 2. Summer, 4. Tourist, 5. Beach, 9. Swimming, 10. Pack, 11. Travel.

Page 43, The Ballet Swan
1. C, 2. D, 3. C, 4. C, 5. Answers will vary.

Page 45, Spirit in Baseball
1. B, 2. A, 3. A, 4. B, 5. D, 6. A, 7. Answers will vary.

Page 46, Baseball Puzzle
Across: 1. Diamond, 3. Bat, 5. Glove, 6. Homerun, 8. Pitcher, 11. Batter; Down: 2. Outs, 3. Bases, 4. Coach, 7. Umpire, 9. Run, 10. Fans.

Page 48, Visitors Poem
1. B, 2. C, 3. B, 4. Answers will vary, 5. Answers will vary.

Page 51, Ski School
1. B, 2. C, 3. A, 4. C, 5. B.

Page 52, Ski School Puzzle Across: 1. Slope, 3. Lift, 5. Instructor, 7. Gloves, 10. School, 11. Ski; Down: 1. Snow, 2. Poles, 4. Boots, 6. Goggles, 8. Mask, 9. Cold.

CHECK YOURSELF, *continued*

Page 54, The Ice Cream Shop
1. B, 2. D, 3. A, 4. C, 5. Answers will vary.

Page 55, Ice Cream Puzzle
Across: 1. Flavors, 3. Dairy, 7. Chocolate, 8. Cone, 9. Shake, 10. Melt; Down: 2. Vanilla, 4. Frozen, 5. Scoop, 6. Dessert.

Page 57, Kelly's Lesson
1. B, 2. C, 3. C, 4. C, 5. A, 6. C.

Page 59, Maggie's New House
1. B, 2. B, 3. C, 4. C.

Page 61, Jessica's New Room
1. D, 2. D, 3. A, 4. C, 5. B, 6. D, 7. A, 8. C.

Page 62, Synonym Puzzle
Across: 2. Grateful, 5. Nice, 6. Carry, 9. Devise, 14. Pitch, 15. Intelligent, 16. Respond, 19. Evening; Down: 1. Navigate, 3. Lean, 4. Firm, 7. Liquid, 8. Raise, 10. Caress, 11. Pretty, 12. Speak, 13. Chilly, 16. Respect, 17. Mean, 18. Fix.

Page 63, Antonym Puzzle
Across: 1. Construct, 2. Broken, 4. Serious, 6. Illustration, 8. Generous, 11. Pillar, 14. Rude, 15. Complicated, 16. Happy, 17. Real; Down: 1. Coarse, 3. Obvious, 5. Shallow, 7. Different, 9. Enormous, 10. Rapid, 12. Lucky, 13. False.

Page 65, A New Puppy
1. B, 2. C, 3. D, 4. B, 5. B, 6. C.

Page 67, Sarah's Dinner
1. C, 2. B, 3. A, 4. C, 5. A, 6. C.

Page 69, Zoo Helpers
1. B, 2. C, 3. C, 4. C, 5. Answers will vary.

Page 70, Zoo Puzzle
Across: 2. Seal, 5. Mollusk, 6. Parrot, 8. Veterinarian, 10. Monkey, 12. Zebra, 14. Captivity; Down: 1. Habitat, 3. Dolphin, 4. Cage, 7. Giraffe, 9. Elephant, 11. Vertebrate, 12. Zoo, 13. Wild.

Page 71, Christmas
1. A, 2. C, 3. B, 4. D, 5. Answers will vary.

Page 72, The Hike Poem
1. A, 2. B, 3. B, 4. B, 5. Answers will vary.

Page 73, Sand People Poem
1. B, 2. A, 3. B, 4. C, 5. Answers will vary.

Page 75, Valentine Cookies
1. C, 2. C, 3. D, 4. A, 5. C, 6. Answers will vary.

Page 76, School Things Puzzle
Across: 3. Grade. 6. Principal, 7. Student, 9. Test. 11. Bus, 12. Lunch, 13. Homework; Down: 1. Friends, 2. PE, 4. Books, 5. Paper, 6. Pencil, 8. Desk, 10. Teacher.

Page 78, Surfing The Web
1. B, 2. C, 3. A, 4. B, 5. B, 6. A, 7. D, 8. C, 9. B, 10. A.

Page 79, A Visit With Matisse
1. A, 2. D, 3. B, 4. A, 5. B.

Page 80, Have Some Tea
1. A, 2. C, 3. B, 4. C, 5. C.

Page 82, Art Lessons
1. B, 2. C, 3. A, 4. B, 5. C, 6. D, 7. D, 8. A.

Page 84, London
1. D, 2. C, 3. B, 4. C, 5. A, 6. B, 7. C, 8. B.

Page 86, Jimmy's Candy Shop Adventure
1. A, 2. B, 3. C, 4. A, 5. Answers will vary.

Page 87, Candy Puzzle
Across: 3. Lemon, 4. Gumdrop, 8. Butterscotch, 9. Peppermint, 10. Taffy; Down: 1. Chocolate, 2. Sugar, 5. Pecan, 6. Grape, 7. Strawberry

Page 89, Natalie's Secret Place
1. A, 2. C, 3. D, 4. B, 5. A, 6. D, 7. B, 8. D.

Page 90, Science Matters
1. F, 2. O, 3. F, 4. O, 5. O, 6. O, 7. O, 8. O, 9. O.

Page 92, Daniel's Holiday
1. B, 2. D, 3. A, 4. B, 5. B, 6. Answer will vary.

Page 94, Mile High City
1. B, 2. C, 3. C, 4. C, 5. A, 6. A, 7. B, 8. C.